A SALUTE TO ANN ALDRICH

If you were a lesbian in the 1950s, you were probably married, with children. Or solitary, drudging in the hinterlands. . . . Could you be the only woman on the planet with tender feelings for other women? Were you evil? Cursed? Or merely sick? . . . And then a miracle happened. In the drug store, the train station, the bus stop, the newsstand, you came across a rack of pulp paperbacks. Among the cowboy tales, the cops-and-robbers, and the science fiction, there began to be books about lesbians. Suddenly, you had a name, an identity, and a community of unknown sisters. . . .

Some of the books you read so eagerly, so secretly, were fictional romances, and even with their heartaches, they provided solace and erotic transport. But another genre appeared: factual reports about lesbian life in the big city, penned by someone who lived there and knew. Her name was Ann Aldrich, and two of her best-known books—*We Walk Alone* and *We, Too, Must Love*—are now being reissued.

Aldrich told you what it was like to come out (joyful prospect!). She told you where lesbians in the know gathered— the bars, the resorts, the restaurants. She told you what these women wore, how they talked, how they coped with intricate personal problems. You were amazed to discover that there were different lifestyles within the nascent lesbian community: high and low, butch and femme, uptown and low-down.

There were even men in the lives of many of them. How did that work? It was a veritable Michelin Guide. You were riveted to the page. . . .

The effect on women was electric. From every corner of creation, they wrote wrenching letters of relief and gratitude. Some were saved from suicide, the only solution to their dilemma they could conceive. Aldrich herself was taken aback at the outpouring of emotion.

—Ann Bannon,
author of *Odd Girl Out* and *The Beebo Brinker Chronicles*
July 2006

Other Works by Ann Aldrich:
We Walk Alone (1955)
Carol in a Thousand Cities (1960)
We Two Won't Last (1963)
Take a Lesbian to Lunch (1972)

WE,
TOO,
MUST
LOVE

ANN ALDRICH

Introduction by Marijane Meaker
Afterword by Stephanie Foote

The Feminist Press
at the City University of New York
New York

Published by the Feminist Press at the City University of New York
The Graduate Center
365 Fifth Avenue
New York, NY 10016
www.feministpress.org

First Feminist Press Edition, 2006.

Originally published by Fawcett Publications in 1958.

Library of Congress Cataloging-in-Publication Data

Aldrich, Ann, 1927 May 27-
  We, too, must love / Ann Aldrich ; introduction by Marijane Meaker ;
afterword by Stephanie Foote. -- 1st Feminist Press ed.
     p. cm.
  Original ed. 1955 by Ann Aldrich.
  ISBN-13: 978-1-55861-527-4 (pbk.)
  ISBN-10: 1-55861-527-x (pbk.)
  ISBN-13: 978-1-55861-528-1(library)
  ISBN-10: 1-55861-528-8 (library)
  1. Lesbians--United States. 2. Lesbianism--United States. I. Title.
HQ75.6.U5A43 2006
306.76'630973--dc22
                              2006021211

This publication was made possible, in part, through the support of
Diane Bernard in honor of Joan R. Heller, Don Linn, and Dorothy Sander and
Joyce Warshow.

Text design by Lisa Force
Printed in Canada by Transcontinental Printing

10 09 08 07 06   5 4 3 2 1

CONTENTS

INTRODUCTION TO THE 2006 EDITION

In 1958, Dick Carroll, my editor at Gold Medal Books, asked me to write the second book in what he saw as the Ann Aldrich series.

We Walk Alone, the original Aldrich, had been inspired by Edward Sagarin, who had used the pseudonym Donald Webster Cory on *The Homosexual in America*. Cory's groundbreaking book was a very thorough examination of the life of a homosexual male. It had no lesbian counterpart. As a young writer of successful paperbacks, my bestseller was a lesbian story, *Spring Fire* (1952), which I had written that under the name Vin Packer.

Pseudonyms were not uncommon in the fifties, particularly if you were writing about homosexuals. I have always liked disguises, and I did not mind at all writing under that name. But I had an altogether different reason for writing under a pseudonym in those days. I had been unable to find a literary agent when I first arrived in New York City, upon my graduation from the University of Missouri. After many attempts to interest an agent in my work, I finally realized that I should become one, and my clients would all be me, with different names. I wrote everything from stories for confession magazines and slicks to suspense novels for Gold Medal Books.

The Vin Packer name had received some attention in the Mystery/Suspense field, with reviews in both the Sunday *New*

York Times, and the Sunday *Herald Tribune*. I had decided the Packer name should stay exclusive to the mystery genre.

Ann Aldrich was the name I chose for my lesbian series, since my editor insisted on a good old American plain Jane name. He wanted nothing fancy or exotic, when I was to appeal to the small town lesbian, the kind of young woman who wrote letters to Vin Packer after she published her first book.

Dick was surprised, the executives at Fawcett were amazed, and even I was incredulous when *Spring Fire* sold 1,463,917 copies. None of us had expected such a response, and the mail for Ms. Packer was largely from small towns all around the United States.

We were not really surprised when Ann Aldrich received even more mail. Although Packer's name was never associated with *We Walk Alone*, the first Aldrich book, it had become obvious that there was a vast lesbian audience.

The territory I knew best, as a lesbian, was New York City. I knew a lot about small town lesbianism, and about being a lesbian in a small town in upstate New York. And I knew quite a bit about being a lesbian in boarding school and college. But most of that experience was undercover. For all those young lesbians who are "out" today, the great majority of us in the fifties were "in." I think those who wrote letters to Ann Aldrich were courageous, for it was the time of witch-hunts and congressional investigations. But they were also the days when a lesbian was often desperate to connect to someone like herself, no matter the risk. Today a lesbian can use any search engine on her computer to find Internet sites, clubs, magazines, newspapers, and television shows catering to her. In the 1950s, you found others by word-of-mouth, by going to bars, and by happenstance.

When I had just graduated from college, and was working for $32.50 a week at a New York publishing house, I found my first gay bar by asking a taxi driver where there was one.

The second Aldrich book, *We, Too, Must Love* had one of

the oddest covers I'd ever seen. The naked women were back-to-back like Siamese twins, perched atop what looked like a red comforter. Someone at Fawcett publications had managed to get a blurb from Dr. Richard Hoffman, recommending the book as "An honest book, a book necessary to light up the dark places of our society."

Praise from an authority of some sort was necessary, for paperback publishers were still shaken by recent postal inspections that banned any books suspected of endorsing an immoral life. Distributing these books was not an easy feat in those days. Some places would not sell them. At the time Packer and Aldrich were just beginning their careers, even I was reluctant to buy my own books, in my Upper East Side friendly tobacco store.

The mail Aldrich received for *We Walk Alone* was a good guide to what readers wanted to know. A majority of my correspondents wanted to move to New York City. Because they asked many questions about where lesbians could find jobs, where they could find bars, and where they could live, I decided to begin there in *We, Too, Must Love*.

I described the Greenwich Village clique and the uptown one. I described beaches and summer resorts, everything from Riis Park to Fire Island. Since my friends and many lesbians I knew all had close male buddies, mostly gay themselves, I wrote about them. I told of business parties where these men became our "beards," or we became theirs. When mothers and fathers visited, we often played our roles again as "dates," or "lovers," and often we went to restaurants and theaters together because we were more comfortable on weekend nights looking like everyone else: boy/girl, boy/girl.

I wrote about lesbians in analysis. There were few "therapists" in those days. Most analysts were MDs and most had Freudian training. Homosexuality was believed to be an abnormality, and those treating us held out little hope for cure.

In addition, many analysands were required to abstain from homosexual sex while in treatment.

In my mail, as in my lesbian life in Manhattan, there were married women. Some claimed to be just curious and others claimed they had been forced to marry to avoid living a life alienated from friends and family. Others played it both ways, and we were all used to the occasional woman who came to bars late at night when her husband was away and her children were being babysat.

One of my chapters in the second Aldrich book deals with drinking. It was a big part of lesbian life (not many of us called it "gay" life back then; the word was just coming into favor). Since most of us went to bars to mingle with or find friends, as well as to look for love, drinking was almost indigenous to the life. There were no lesbian clubs holding dances for us, and no homosexual community centers offering entertainment. We were relegated to crummy bars run by the Mafia, who in turn had to pay off the police so we wouldn't be arrested and hauled off to jail in the paddy wagon. (Many times we were, anyway.) A blink of the lights told customers the police were at the door. All same-sex dancing had to stop immediately.

If both of my parents were not already dead, surely a glance at Sunday's *New York Times* Styles section with its same-sex wedding announcements would quickly do them in.

We have come a long way from the Manhattan days of Ms. Aldrich and her lesbian friends and lovers.

We, Too, Must Love is a testament to the tyranny of the old mores, some of which still exist today. It is also a testament to the perseverance, ingenuity, and ultimate triumph of those whose sexual orientation isn't the same as the majority. But we must always remember that as long as certain laws rule against us, and some religions consider us an abomination, we are not equal to our oppressors.

Marijane Meaker
East Hampton
2006

FOREWORD

In 1955 I wrote a book called *We Walk Alone*, a study of the Lesbian, by a Lesbian. After its publication, I received hundreds of letters. Doctors wrote; mothers and fathers of Lesbians wrote; girls who weren't sure whether or not they were Lesbians wrote, and girls wrote who knew that they were. I found my mail almost totally lacking in frivolity. I read letters from angry people, frightened people, grateful people, sad people, and a vast number from people who wanted to know more about the female homosexual.

Among these letters there was this one from Houston, Texas:

> *I have just finished reading* We Walk Alone, *and I want to get some of my thoughts about your book down on paper. First, thank you—thank you for writing it. It was not a very happy book, but it was a badly needed one.*
>
> *When I read the chapter "A Word to Parents," I thought of myself ten years ago, when I very crudely, and defensively (and foolishly!) tried to make up for my folks' finding out about me, by blaming them. I thought: How much simpler if I could have given them a book like yours, and said: "This is what I am. It's not pretty, but it's true, and I want you to understand me."*

When I read the chapter on Greenwich Village, I thought: *If I had only read that while I was living down there—instead of learning its bitter truth through four years of misery. Maybe it would have lessened the time. Maybe I would have seen what I was becoming.*

When I read the chapter on how a Lesbian becomes what she is, things began to come back to me—little things about how I was as a kid. I began to see myself more clearly. I used to think I didn't want to put myself under a microscope and see my real nature, but, Miss Aldrich, thank God I did. I think sometimes we are too self-pitying, too ready to blame society for our personalities, and not very often willing to admit our faults.

I'm glad you didn't try to whitewash us—try to say we're perfectly normal. I'm glad you pointed out we bring a lot of trouble on ourselves. At the same time, I'm glad you explained to people that we're not all tough, trouser-wearing, cropped-hair, aggressive women who hate men and flaunt our ways; but that like any other group, we're made up of many, many complex and different personalities.

I wished there were more to We Walk Alone! I hope some day you'll write another book like it, maybe a sequel.

It's been a long time since I've been to New York, and lately I'd begun to think I'd regret my decision to move away and divorce myself from the "gay" life there, but your book let me know I'd made the right choice.

I have a good job here, and good friends, and at last I'm beginning to find some of that happiness I'd sought for so long. You've contributed to it, Miss Aldrich, and again—thank you.

Sincerely yours,
Marjorie T.

This book is not only an answer to that letter, and to all the others, but it is a supplement to *We Walk Alone*. In it, I shall write of the facets and foibles of homosexual life as I have known it in New York City—and of the women and girls involved in it.

New York City, in a sense, is a focal point. Just as a scientist can often know more about the whole by studying the isolated part offering the most potential, I think so can more be known about the female homosexual by studying one of her most populated habitats.

As a Lesbian, I shall act as a reporter within my own group and those groups with which I am familiar.

In the last chapter I shall leave the discussion to give a more elaborate description of the mail I received. I believe this may point up much of the current opinion on the subject, and crystallize for the reader the prevalent ignorance about the Lesbian—in many cases on the part of the Lesbian herself. It should also illustrate the dire need for dissemination of knowledge about the female variant—who she is, what she is, and how she can be helped by competent authorities, and a sympathetic disposition toward her plight on the part of the public.

My purpose in writing this book is to dispel much of the ignorance which stems mainly from lack of information about the Lesbian. It is not my intention to endorse or to condemn a way of life which is abnormal, but merely to reveal it, with the hope for broader understanding.

Ann Aldrich
New York
1958

Dear Miss Aldrich:

I am at the point of suicide. I honestly mean that. I am one of those transvestites you write about. If you were to see me on the street, you'd think I was a man. I really don't look like a woman at all.

Where I live they know what I am, and I'm the town joke. My sister calls me a lady-lover.

I don't want your sympathy. I don't know exactly what I do want, but I found a copy of your book in the drugstore and I suppose I just want to say thanks for writing that book.

It doesn't help me, but maybe it'll keep some kid from being like me if she reads it in time, or if her folks do.

M. L.
Dayton, Ohio

1.   TOGETHERNESS

A young furniture salesman told me the following incident, which took place during the convention week of the furniture manufacturers in Chicago. He had taken to dinner the designer of the line he was selling, a rather beautiful girl in her late twenties called Paula.

Bill had known Paula for about three years. They had traveled back and forth to Chicago, and Grand Rapids, and Philadelphia, on business; he had visited her at her apartment, and often had dinner and lunch with her. They were very friendly, and being a married man, he had often teased her, asking when she was going to get married. She had shrugged, or laughed, or answered that she hadn't found the right man.

That evening they had had many drinks, and at one point, Bill's eyes fell to the watch she was wearing. It was a sports watch, which was out of place with the white silk sheath she was wearing. The black leather strap was worn; the loop broken. The watch looked large as a man's watch.

When Bill raised his eyes from her wrist, she looked into them momentarily, as if to read his thoughts, and then said with a faint grin: "Ugly, isn't it?"

He smiled. "It doesn't look much like you."

"Yes it does, and I've always worn it."

"I never noticed before," Bill said.

"A woman gave it to me," she told him. She was a little high by then. Her voice was thick and she had trouble lighting her cigarette, before Bill could scratch a match and light it for her. Then she said, "She had the back engraved. It says: *Not Impossible* on the back."

"What does that mean?"

"That it's completely impossible."

"I don't get it," Bill said. "What is it that's impossible?"

"For two women to stay together," Paula answered. "At least it was for Carla and me."

"Was she your roommate?"

"Nothing as permanent as all that," Paula said. "She was my lover."

Bill took a swallow of whisky. He couldn't think of anything to say to that.

"By now Carla has a rather negative approach to the whole idea anyway," Paula continued. "She went with Betty Allen for about three years. You know, the singer. Then she went with some woman who ran a mink farm. And then an actress. Ever heard of Eleanor Scott?"

Bill hadn't.

"No reason why you should have. She's in off-Broadway things mostly. Does some television too. After Carla and she broke up, and after Carla and I broke up, then Scott and I tried." Paula smiled. "It's like Hands-Around, isn't it?"

"But Paula," Bill said, "how come all these—these—" He fumbled for a more subtle word.

"Lesbians," Paula said.

"Yes. How come they all know each other? Do they live in Greenwich Village?"

"Oh, Bill, come *on*!"

"Well, I don't know anything about it. I mean, I've never even thought about it . . . or that you were," he added weakly.

Paula said, "I read a book once, by a purported Lesbian

named Ann Aldrich. It was called *We Walk Alone*. She claimed she'd been one for fifteen years, yet she'd never been able to spot another Lesbian in a crowd. No wonder she walks alone."

"Can you spot one, Paula?"

"Oh, not *always*, of course. Most of the time, particularly in New York. You get signals, some as obvious as klieg lights, others more subtle. A certain way of letting their eyes meet yours and hold for a second or so; I always call that 'the long drink.' Or an arch to the eyebrow. Or a particular tip to the mouth, almost a smile but not a smile. And, naturally, some by what they wear or say, or the general way they act."

Bill said, "And then what happens? Do you—I mean, do you—"

"Go to bed?"

Bill nodded.

Paula said, "Usually not. Hardly ever. But if you're working in the same office, or you've met at the same party, or something like that, you might make arrangements to see each other. If you're already involved with someone, you might have your new acquaintance over to dinner, and tell her to bring someone. Lots of times she brings someone she's involved with. You all get to know each other."

"Like a sorority, eh?" Bill said.

"Sort of," Paula smiled. "It's togetherness, you know— birds of a feather and all that. And because in the *Twilight World*, as the copywriters would say—things are so ephemeral it's as practical as instant coffee. When it comes time for one of us to find a new face, we just get up and march to the music the way you do in a Paul Jones. When the music stops, everyone's got a new partner."

Bill said, "You sound awfully cynical."

"Sometimes I feel that way," she said. "Sometimes I feel that it's just a choice between the hell or the *Well of Loneliness*."

Much of what Paula said is indigenous to the New York Lesbian with whom this book will deal, for despite the particular clique in which a Lesbian travels in the city, despite their class differences and the differences in their positions, there is a togetherness in many of their attitudes and habits which is a common ground.

First—the watch, with its inscription on the back: *Not Impossible* . . . One might well infer from that sentiment that its donor had found in other similar situations that it was impossible. Indeed, Paula told Bill ". . . Carla went with Betty Allen . . . then with someone who ran a mink farm . . . then an actress . . ." before she presented the watch to Paula.

The token gift between Lesbians who are "going together" is a familiar practice; the engraving on the gift is equally familiar. Wedding bands are not infrequently exchanged, and on the inside the initials of the pair, and a date, are inscribed.

One Lesbian, discussing this phenomenon with me, had this to say about it: "Some girls put the date they met inside the rings, but I don't consider that right. Helen and I put the date we started living together inside ours. I don't think you're really serious unless you live together."

Helen, my friend's "girl," has a drawerful of such token gifts left over from previous romances. Among them is a chain bracelet with a gold heart attached to it. On the back of the heart is written: *H. & K. . . . only forever.* There is a Byzantine coin, attached to a leather neck cord. On one side of the coin are the words *Never leave Jackie.* There is a silver little-finger ring with "I. G. A. T. Y. F." inside. Helen told me this was the abbreviation of the title of "their song"— "I've Grown Accustomed To Your Face," and the ring had been given to her by "Mary Francis, who goes with Ginny Roberts now."

It is not uncommon for the metropolitan Lesbian, who travels with a crowd, to have many such tokens—rings, bracelets, charms, crosses, Stars of David, and whatnot, left over from the past. Old photographs of former lovers, old love letters and souvenirs are often saved.

Why? Perhaps part of the answer is contained in what the designer, Paula, had told my friend Bill: ". . . When it comes time for one of us to find a new face, we just get up and march to the music the way you do in a Paul Jones. When the music stops, everyone's got a new partner." The cynicism which Bill sensed is understandable. The ephemeralness of which she complained is a standard complaint. This is illustrated in the response of a friend to whom I remarked: "Why do you say Barbara and Kelly are different?"

My friend said: "Isn't that pretty obvious! After all, they've been together four and a half years!" Four and a half years is con-sidered a pretty obvious indication that these particular Lesbians are exceptional. My friend's added comment throws even more light on the matter. She said, "And the whole while, neither one strayed. And after all this time, they're still sleeping together."

Lesbians who stay together four yours or longer without straying, and who still maintain a full relationship—for there are many, of whom I shall write in later chapters, who stay together but do not make love together any longer—are defi-nitely the exception. Perhaps this is the reason they keep the souvenirs of their former romances—perhaps to say:

"This is when I went with Ann! Ann was beautiful, and here is proof she loved me once!"

Or: "Look what Tony had engraved on this coin! Tony was really sensitive and loving."

Or: "Here's the watch Karen gave me. She never cared about the price. I meant the world to her."

And to whom are they saying these things, by holding on to their souvenirs? To the girls they go with now, to remind them they've been loved before—"better loved," in case of argument and to the girls they might go with in the future, should anything happen to the present relationship; and they say these things to themselves. For like the restless young rock-'n'-roll seductress, or the voluptuous Hollywood actress, or any young girl or woman who cannot yet completely count on one love for the rest of her life, the proof that there have been many loves is necessary for the ego.

A modern bride discards her souvenirs when she marries, or leaves them back in some old trunk at Mother's. The "gay" girl, about to enter a relationship simulating a marriage, with another girl, is usually reluctant to discard her souvenirs, and wouldn't dare leave them with Mother. She may put them away, but she most always brings them with her.

Among many Lesbians in New York, the girl they "went with before" is a feather in their cap.

I've often heard a Lesbian ask this kind of question of another Lesbian at a party: "Who did that redhead over there in the corner by herself—that Judy Random—who did she go with before?"

"With Pat Pryce," the answer might be.

And the one who asked, eyebrows raising with pleasure, smiling, might say, "Really!" in that slow, I'll-consider-it tone.

Social climbing the Lesbian ladder will be dealt with in a future chapter; in some instances, possessing a ring or a love letter from the right person is sufficient dowry for a gay "marriage" to another Lesbian.

"I'm going with Sue Lys," one Lesbian might tell another, and without any further elaboration on who Sue is or what Sue does, she will add: "Sue went with Mary Lee White, you know."

Another point brought out in Bill's conversation with the designer, was that of being able to recognize a Lesbian. Among a good majority of the female homosexuals in New York City, there is this feeling. As Paula herself told Bill, some signs are as obvious as klieg lights, others more subtle.

In my own experience, I reiterate the opinion I expressed

in *We Walk Alone*, which Paula criticized. With the exception of the Lesbians in gay bars, or the transvestites on the street, I have never been able to pick a Lesbian out of a crowd, if she did not communicate with me by some direct means, such as the searching look, or the "certain" conversation. Often when Lesbians are together, their manner, their dress, and their general attitude may lead one to suspect that they are Lesbians. And often, one woman may wonder if another is a Lesbian, like herself, and may try to find out by talking with her.

Too often, Lesbians might imagine that they can "tell" another.

"Cruising" is a word more indigenous to the world of male homosexuality than to the Lesbian world, but cruising does exist in the Lesbian's world. The word has many overtones, and ambiguities. In some cases it means to go out and hunt a partner. In others it means to go to the gay bars and see what's going on and to mix with other gay people. Cruising can also mean looking someone over at a party, in the office, or on the street, wondering if she is homosexual.

The latter sort of cruising is often the sort that prompts the Lesbian to exaggerate her powers of perception. One afternoon I was with another Lesbian in a department store.

"This is a fantastic place!" she exclaimed, "It's so 'cruisy' today. Everyone is 'coming on.'"

"Coming on?" I said.

"Don't you notice it? I've been looked straight at, up-and-down, by about a dozen women from the perfume counter on up to bedding. It's a camp!"

Another friend described her new boss to me this way:

"She may wear a wedding ring and go home every night to her husband, but she cruises me like mad. She has a certain way of resting her hand on my shoulder when she leans over my desk, and that smile she gives me—with those eyes needling mine!"

In some instances, a Lesbian can actually detect the interest of another Lesbian in a public place; or she may not be really a Lesbian, but a woman who is conscious of another woman's subtle sexual interest in her which makes her curious. Sometimes such a woman is more than curious—sometimes she is strangely attracted, even though she herself is not homosexual. Many times, however, this imagined ability to spot a gay sister is simply the Lesbian's seeing life around her through the spectacles of her own neurosis.

The habit of dropping names of famous actresses, authoresses, wives of public figures, women in history and in the arts—claiming that they "know for a fact" they are Lesbians, is another habit peculiar to the New York City Lesbian.

One night I was watching television with a group when a well-known young husband-and-wife team performed a duet. While they sang, the conversation went like this:

"You'd never know they were both gay, would you?"

"Are they?"

"Oh, God, yes! I knew a girl who went with her."

"*He* looks it."

"He goes with Tony North, the star."

"No kidding! Is Tony gay, too?"

"Didn't you know that? So's his wife."

"She is?"

"Sure! I thought everyone knew that. She goes with Gabrielle Masters."

"Oh, I knew she was gay."

"Yeah, Gabrielle went with a friend of mine, an actress, for a while out in L. A., but it didn't last."

The homosexual often sounds like an authority on the private lives of celebrities; and all celebrities in their private lives seem to be homosexuals. Whether it is a transvestite "dike" type talking, a Greenwich Village–type talking, or an uptown, East side gay girl talking, she "knows for a fact" that so-and-so is a Lesbian; that she went with this one and that one, and that so-and-so's husband is a faggot.

If there are many things peculiar to most Lesbians in New York City, there are some which distinguish the different cliques of Lesbians. In the next few chapters we will visit those who live downtown in the Village, those who live uptown, and those whose address is less important to them than the way they dress. We will visit them in their bars, at their beaches, at their places of business; in their homes and the homes of their parents.

We will see what it is that attracts the female to the *Well of Loneliness*, and whether or not there is only a choice between that and the hell of loneliness for the Lesbian of Manhattan.

2.   A GIRL COMES OUT

1. On the Boardwalk of Atlantic City

Fortune Secora used to see them every day on the boardwalk.
One was a tall girl with a husky physique and a square-shaped
ruddy, masculine face. She wore her hair only a little longer
than a man's, and she always wore black bermuda shorts with
black knee-length socks, loafers, a man's short-sleeved sports
shirt, and a checkered cap with a belt in the back.

The other girl had the same pitch-black hair, but she wore
it long and feminine, so that it fell to her shoulders and hung
like shimmering coal around her face. Her mouth was wild
and wide, colored sensually with scarlet, good white teeth
showing between slightly parted lips. Her nose was thin,
almost classical, and she had high cheekbones. A black pen-
ciled line and mascaraed lashes delineated her eyes. Her eyes
were wide-set and sparkling brown, flecked with green around
the edges of the irises. They were quiet and warm and bright,
and occasionally they glanced for a moment at Fortune, and
smiled. It used to make Fortune feel strange.

"I was working as a waitress in Atlantic City for the summer," Fortune told me, "hoping to save up enough to go to
New York and get my own apartment. I was eighteen then.
My folks lived in Trenton. I loved my mother, but my old man
was a terror. He never drank or anything like that, but he

believed that sin would destroy me. He was always preaching at me, criticizing me and warning me I wouldn't be around for long. I had to get away."

Fortune was lonely in Atlantic City. She had a small room, where she spent a good deal of her time reading science fiction and mulling over her horoscope. Her name had been coined by her high-school classmates, because Fortune was a strong believer in astrology. It was this belief that led her to speak to the pair of girls she had seen so often on the boardwalk.

"I used to wonder about them," Fortune said, "and particularly about the one with the long black hair. It was so crazy. I didn't even know her, but my life began to revolve around her. I used to wait hours on the boardwalk just to see her pass, and when she noticed me, I'd nearly die. Even when she wasn't anywhere around, I used to imagine that she could see me, or that she was behind me watching me, and I'd get so self-conscious! I always thought one day she'd probably come marching into the restaurant where I was working. I'd probably have dropped a trayful of food!"

Fortune Secora had no way of divining the nature of this obsession with the girl with the long black hair. She supposed it was just another crush. In high school she had had one on her gym teacher. At a girl's camp one year, she had had one on the crafts teacher. But the thought that she might be a Lesbian was farthest from her mind. She had gone steady twice between her freshman and her senior years, and while she knew no young men in Atlantic City, she did think the busboy in the restaurant where she worked was a "doll."

Fortune was a pretty girl. She was thin, of medium height, and had an average figure. At one time she had worried because she was a little flat-chested, but she was certainly not underdeveloped. She wore her curly blonde hair an inch or so below her ears, doing it up in bobby pins every night. Fortune had done her share of kissing and petting, but at eighteen she was a virgin.

"Sometimes I would get very excited with a boy," she told me, "and I'd want to go the limit, but I was too scared. I'd think of my father's preaching, and of his red-hot temper, and I'd be afraid I'd get pregnant and that *he'd* kill me long before Armageddon would."

The hot afternoon in July when Fortune first spoke to the pair of girls, was forecast by her horoscope this way:

P.M. Take advantage of the afternoon to make new friends. Get outside of yourself. You won't be sorry.

Fortune had been standing at a hot-dog stand munching a hamburger, reading this in an astrology magazine, when the pair walked over to the same counter.

Fortune told me, "I was so nervous I couldn't finish the rest of my hamburger, because I was afraid they'd see my hand was shaking. But my horoscope seemed like a sign. I decided to just jump in the way you do sometimes when you're going swimming, and are hesitant about getting wet. I just spoke right up: 'Hello,' I said, 'I've seen you around so much I feel as if we're friends.'"

The girls introduced themselves, and the three of them stood there talking. The one with the long black hair was named Miki. She was a hostess in a nightclub, where Morgan, her friend, was bartender.

"It's a gay club, they told me," Fortune said, "and I told them I wished the place I worked was, but it was real dead. I said no one ever seemed to smile and the tips were terrible. They both began to laugh. They wanted to know if I knew what 'gay' meant. I said sure—happy, fun, jolly. They laughed all the more and I was confused for a while, but not for long."

Morgan and Miki told Fortune all about gay clubs and gay girls. *They* were both gay, they explained. They were going together. They said there were hundreds just like themselves, right there in Atlantic City, and they said that in New York there were thousands. Fortune couldn't believe them at first.

She had read *Well of Loneliness* and that was all she knew about that sort of thing. When she read that book, she said, she just thought the girls in it were nuts.

"I didn't get excited by that book or think I was like them, or any of that. But Miki telling me that she was gay did something to me. I think I was already very much in love with her."

Morgan and Miki had an apartment in Atlantic City which they had been sharing with another girl. When the other girl quit her job and left Atlantic City, they asked Fortune if she wanted to move in with them. It would cut down expenses all the way around, and Fortune would no longer be lonely.

"It was like a heaven and a hell for me," Fortune said. "Being around Miki was heaven. She treated me like a kid sister. I never had anyone treat me so warmly. She'd call me 'honey' and 'darling' and she'd warn any gay kids who came to the place to leave me alone because I was straight. She'd tease me about the busboy at the place where I worked, and she'd tell me that some day I'd marry a handsome man and raise a big family. She didn't know how I loved her . . . Loving her the way I did and watching Morgan kiss her, and watching Morgan and her so loving together, was hell. Another thing—I was afraid to undress around her, or let her see me half undressed. She just inhibited me something awful. It was the most peculiar thing that had ever happened to me."

Secretly Fortune wrote poems about Miki. One day Miki found this one between the pages of a book Fortune was reading:

Earthbound

When I see your eyes,
I soar, climb, touch stars singing your name,
Whirl momentarily in the blue heavens and cry for love,
Before the return to earth.

Then on the ground, I look at the sky that was mine,
And know it was no more mine than you are.
I say, "Miki," but it is not a song, or a cry;
Simply a word anyone can say.
"Miki" I say, but I need your eyes
To give it wings.

Fortune told me Miki said to her:

"You don't love me. You just have a thing on me, kid. You're not gay. Don't think that for a minute. You stay straight. Get married, and don't get mixed up in this life."

But Fortune was far too lovesick to listen to Miki. All she could think about was Miki, and the one thing she wanted to do then, was to "come out." She had heard Morgan and Miki use that expression. When a girl "came out" she had her first homosexual love experience. Sometimes two fairly innocent girls found each other and made love to each other, and that way came out together. But more often an experienced Lesbian brought another girl out.

Fortune believed that if she could come out Miki might return her love, but as long as she was still straight, Miki would not touch her.

"I wasn't Miki's type at all," Fortune said, "but I was too hung up in love to care. I was hung by my toenails. Miki liked strong, masculine girls who would boss her around and act like men, and I was a little cream-puff, but I didn't think about it. I just wanted Miki to love me. I guess all those kids in Atlantic City knew what I was going through—even Morgan. They felt sorry for me."

One night at a party, near the end of the summer, Fortune had her chance to come out.

"I went with Miki and Morgan and a bunch of others, up to the inlet, after work, for some drinks. There was this very masculine girl eying me all the time. Her name was Tommy. She was kind of like Morgan, and I wasn't at all attracted to her, but she was to me. She had a room near the inlet and she asked me to go there with her. Miki said she'd break my neck if I did, but I wanted to make Miki jealous; I wanted to show her I was not straight. I went with Tommy. When she kissed me I didn't feel excited. She was too masculine, and when she undressed, she was wearing men's jockey shorts. It looked dumb for a girl to be wearing men's underwear, and I didn't like it. I got a funny feeling from the whole thing. I knew something physical had happened to me for the first time, but I felt dirty because I didn't really like Tommy. I got out of there as fast as I could and went back to the apartment to find Miki. She was wonderful to me. She rocked me in her arms like a baby, and told me I'd find my own girl some day, someone I could love who would love me."

From that summer on, Fortune has lived in the gay world. When you see her in the bars wearing men's pants and shoes and shirts, with her hair cut short and combed back, you see what might be a young boy. Unlike Morgan, or Tommy, Fortune is not a complete transvestite. She owns no men's suits or sports coats, no ties or male underwear. When she works at the restaurant as a waitress, she wears a skirt, combs her hair in a more feminine style, and looks much like any other girl.

After she came to New York with Miki and Morgan, she did find a girl of her own. She met her in a gay club in the Village, and "brought her out." The girl was one of many—from the Bronx, Queens, Brooklyn, or from Washington Heights—who come in groups to homosexual haunts to see what it's all about.

"Sometimes," Fortune told me, "I wonder if I'd be gay now if I hadn't met Morgan and Miki. I think I would; it was bound to come out in me. If I hadn't, I might be married now, and have children. I don't think I'd have made a very good wife

or mother. You see, I never had much of love, not real affectionate love. Because of my father, I'm afraid of men, afraid to
loosen up with them. Even in high school, when I was going
steady, I never said 'darling' or 'honey' to my boy friend. I was
sort of cold. I liked to kiss them, but I was never my real self.
With Patty, my girl friend, I can express myself. I'm always
writing her poems and stuff. I wouldn't do that with a man."

Patty added: "The fellows I know don't write poetry. They
think it's mush. They're all clucks. Rough and only after one
thing. Fortune is tender and sweet. When she brought me out
she kept saying 'Stop me any time if you don't want me to
touch you any more.' A man wouldn't say that!"

2. On Charles Street, Apartment 3-C . . .

Jackie always knew about herself, but she never dared do anything about it. On the contrary, she did her very best to disprove
the fact by having many affairs with men, by choosing only the
most feminine of girls for her companions in college, and by
reacting with feigned revulsion at any mention of homosexuality.

Jackie used to say: "I just can't see anything remotely
attractive about a woman's body. The male body is exciting
and beautiful, but the female's leaves me cold."

She made it sound very convincing. None of the three
sorority sisters with whom she came to New York City after college, would ever dream that Jacqueline Spencer was a Lesbian.
On the large Midwest campus where they were at college
together, Jackie had been pinned to a Sigma Chi for a while, and
to a Beta for a longer time. She had made it very clear that she
was not a virgin, and she often went into rapturous-sounding
descriptions of her love-making with men. If anything, Jackie
was considered a little fast with the boys; a little boy-crazy.

Jacqueline told me, "Since I was a kid I knew something
was wrong with me. I was always in love with girls. There's just
no sense in calling them crushes. I was violently in love with

them, and in my daydreams I was always kissing them and touching their bodies. When I was about thirteen I found an old medical book in our library at home, and it was in that book that I first saw the word "homosexual." The moment I read what a homosexual was I said to myself: That's me. I did everything I could to keep anyone from suspecting. My folks never did. I think one or two of the girls I was in love with did, because once or twice I tried to kiss them, and they acted hostile to me afterwards. When I would see them at dances in the school gym, I would get a boy friend to dance me by them, and I would hold real close to him and close my eyes and behave as though we were madly in love. I think that's what started me sleeping with boys. I wanted a reputation for being very sexy with men.

"In college I joined a sorority. I was very deeply in love with the president. Once I had to appear before her for being out after hours with a man. She nearly cried. I think she felt something for me too. She said: 'Jacqueline, why are you doing this to us?' By 'us' she meant the sorority, but the way she said it, and the tears in her eyes, made me cry too. We just wept together. When I think back on it now, I wish I'd tried to kiss her as I wanted to. The men I dated were all nice guys, but I didn't love them. I could never love a man, and I knew it."

The four sorority sisters came to New York and got an apartment in Greenwich Village. Jackie wanted to be a writer. She took an evening job as an airlines reservation clerk, so that she could use the days to write. The apartment the girls had was on the third floor, in the rear, overlooking a garden.

"There was a young couple living on the first floor, and I would watch them in their garden. The husband was very good-looking, and the wife was beautiful. She dressed a very special way—tapered slacks, sandals, beautiful madras shirts, and her hair pulled back off her shoulders and held by a silver bandeau. She had a sort of sophisticated look. My landlady said her husband was an actor and she was a photographer. I was fascinated by them and used to watch them all the time, but my eye was usually on her. She used to see me standing in my window, and wave to me. They both used to speak to me in the hall, in a very friendly way.

"One night late when I came home from work, my room-mates were huddled together around the window and gig-gling. They told me that the people downstairs were having a party in their garden, and that women were dancing with women, and men were dancing with men. I went and looked out. Japanese lanterns were strung up, and a young man was playing an accordion. What my friends reported was true. I pretended to be as shocked as my roommates, but my heart was beating like a drum.

"About a week after that I met the woman in the grocery store one morning. We walked home together and introduced ourselves. Her name was Cynthia Fullerton. She asked me in for some iced tea. The apartment was fabulous. Photographs she'd taken lined the walls, and everything was special. There was a bowl of litchi nuts on the coffee table, and a beautiful Japanese wind bell hung in the window. She had a huge record collection, and a hi-fi set she'd built herself. While we drank iced tea she played some records, and told me about the won-derful year she and her husband spent in Mexico.

"When I went back upstairs, I was dizzy with it all. I was head over heels in love with her. I told my roommates when they came home that I'd met her. 'Is she a Lesbian?' one want-ed to know. 'Did she try to kiss you?'

"They all made jokes about it, and I was furious. I told them a lie. I said she told me all about her party the other night—that her husband had had to entertain some of his 'queer' theatrical friends, and that she was horrified by them. They weren't too ready to believe me, particularly as I saw more and more of Cynthia.

"We were together every morning. Tony, her husband, never seemed to mind. He liked me. When he was there, we were a happy threesome. When he wasn't, Cynthia and I got along as though we'd known each other all our lives. She never once mentioned the subject of homosexuality, but by that time I knew she felt the way I did. She would reach out and touch my cheek with her fingers when we were together, and she always sat as close to me as she could. She called me 'Sweet,' and she often said, 'Ah, Jackie, how did we ever find each other!'

"One morning when I went down to see her she was still in bed. She shouted at me to come on in. I went back to the bedroom and she was there in the bed, just looking at me. I didn't say anything. I just went over and sat by her. We looked at each other for a minute, and then I don't know who did what, but all of a sudden, we were in each other's arms. That was the beginning of everything for me.

"Two months later I decided to move downstairs with her. Tony knew all about us. He was a homosexual himself. He said he'd get a place of his own. When I told my roommates they were sick about it. I knew they'd guessed what had happened to me, but they never said anything right out. Just as I was leaving, though, with my bags all packed, I said: 'Gee, I'll be right downstairs, we can see a lot of each other.'

"One of them said, 'You come up here if you want to see us.'

"I asked her, 'Don't you like Cyn?'

"'No,' she said, 'not that kind of *sin*.'"

Jacqueline Spencer's sorority sisters are all married now and have moved away from Greenwich Village. Jacqueline still lives in the Village. Through Cynthia she met the Village clique of Lesbians; she has gone with several of the girls in that clique since then.

"When I came out," she says, "I came into my own. I found my slot. I was home! If it hadn't been for Cynthia, I'd probably have been through the divorce courts half a dozen times, given birth to some unhappy children, and drunk myself to death in the end. Finally, I have some self-respect!"

3. Off Fifth in the Eighties . . .

"How about dinner tonight?" Huguette's boss said suddenly one afternoon. "I'll treat you. You've been working so hard."

Huguette was a French girl who had been in this country less than a year. She'd been lucky to find this job, which she had had for two months. Her boss was a woman, a press agent in her late thirties, and Huguette was more or less a Gal Friday. The pay was fair, and Miss Taylor was very patient with her shorthand, which she was attending night school to improve.

Huguette was thrilled by the invitation. She admired Miss Taylor tremendously, though she was sometimes a little afraid of her. Miss Taylor was an energetic, handsome, dynamic individual with a brusque voice and a quick temper. But when she wanted to be, she was charming.

That evening she wanted to be.

In her Volkswagon, she drove Huguette to Tarrytown. In a fabulous terrace tower of a restaurant there, they sipped cocktails high above the Hudson River.

Miss Taylor wanted to be called what everyone called her—Tay—and she wanted to know all about Huguette.

Huguette told her. She was twenty-two. Her older sister had married an American doctor, and after a few years, she had arranged for Huguette to come to this country. The working conditions were better here, and the salaries were higher. Maybe Huguette would be able to save enough to return to France eventually, and go through college.

Huguette lived in the Evangeline Home on West 13th Street. It was inexpensive, she had a room to herself, and she had made many nice friends.

"And what about boy friends?" Miss Taylor wondered.

"I would like to meet a rich one," Huguette laughed.

"One who could afford something like this."

Miss Taylor made a great impression on her Gal Friday that night. Huguette had never been outside of the city for dinner; never been to such an expensive restaurant; never tasted moules marinière like that anywhere outside of France. The wine with dinner was the finest; the brandy afterward enough to make Huguette choke up with nostalgia, and the ride home under the stars in the light of a half-moon, with a Chopin concerto playing over the radio, was just like the movies.

Miss Taylor dropped her off in front of the Evangeline Home. "We'll do it again some time," she promised.

That night Huguette did not sleep well. Time and time again her thoughts returned to the evening—to the smart red car with the top down, to the breathtaking view of the river, to the pop of the cork in the wine bottle, and the way the waiter very correctly poured some into a glass to be tasted and approved before continuing to pour; to the clink of the crystal brandy snifters as Miss Taylor touched hers to Huguette's; and to the stars, and Chopin, and the lights of the George Washington Bridge in the distance. It would be nice to live like that always—it would be fabulous!

Swollen-eyed from lack of sleep, groggy, Huguette went to work the next morning. When she filed a letter in the wrong place, Miss Taylor exploded: "Do you think I pay you for nothing! I just won't tolerate mistakes like that!"

When Miss Taylor stormed out to lunch, Huguette wept.

"I wanted her approval so much," Huguette said. "She was so strong—like my father, so stern! I was frightened by her, but she was the one person I wanted to have like me."

After another week passed, Miss Taylor asked Huguette if she would like to see *My Fair Lady*. She had press passes. The play had been on Broadway only a few weeks, and everyone was trying to get tickets to it. Huguette was overwhelmed.

Miss Taylor said they would have a bite to eat after the

show. Huguette hurried around locating the original reviews of the musical, so that afterward, when they talked together, she would say the right things. She fussed over what she would wear, and spent some of her savings for a new hat.

"I wanted so badly to look and act perfect that night," she said, "I felt I had to impress her. When I arrived at the theater she was standing out front waiting for me. The first words she said were: 'The hat has to go.' She checked the hat, and said I could pick it up tomorrow. She said I shouldn't wear hats, that New Yorkers just *didn't*. I felt this big!"

After the theater, Miss Taylor took Huguette to Sardi's. They ate downstairs. There was very little time to talk, since the pair were constantly interrupted by people who knew Tay. One woman, a female vocalist whose records Huguette had often heard, said to Miss Taylor: "Who's the new face?" She smiled and winked at Huguette.

Miss Taylor told the woman: "Hands off."

Huguette was never sure why she felt suddenly proud at that moment.

"It was as though I was protected by this strong woman," Huguette said; "but protected from what I didn't think."

After that night, Huguette watched closely how Miss Taylor dressed and tried to emulate her. She listened to Miss Taylor's opinions, and they became hers. When Miss Taylor was angry, she cowered; when Miss Taylor was happy, Huguette beamed; when Miss Taylor seemed remotely pleased with Huguette, Huguette's spirits soared.

There were other evenings out, more trips to the theater. Huguette found herself refusing to make plans with anyone right up until the last minute, and sometimes past it—hoping Miss Taylor would say the familiar words: "Do you have anything scheduled for this evening?"

One evening Huguette was asked to a party at Miss Taylor's home, in the East Eighties, off Fifth.

"She said just a few old friends were dropping in," Huguette recounted the experience, "but when I got there, there must have been fifty people—clients, actresses, singers, and dancers, and others—women and men I'd never met before. Everyone was drinking a lot. Miss Taylor was too. At one point she played the score to *My Fair Lady*. In front of everyone there, she looked at me and said: 'Remember, baby?' Then she sang from one of the songs, making an innovation on the words:

> *"I was extremely independent and content*
> *until we met*
> *Surely I will always be that way, and yet,*
> *Huguette*
> *I've grown accustomed to your face . . ."*

Everyone laughed, but Huguette could feel her cheeks burn. Somebody said: "She's actually blushing! That is refreshing."

Miss Taylor came over to her and drew her aside: "I have, you know," she said. "Do you want to wait until everyone goes. I'll drive you home."

"Somehow I knew then and there that I would spend the night with her," Huguette said, "and I'd never wanted anything more in my whole life."

Huguette added: "As everyone was leaving, that woman who had come up to us in Sardi's said to me: 'Well, congratulations, little Miss France. Looks like you've finally hooked her!'"

3. WHY CAN'T A WOMAN BE MORE LIKE A MAN?

In *The Hearth and the Strangeness* by N. Martin Kramer, the Lesbian, Aliciane, tells of how she came to acquire that trait of homosexual thinking mentioned in my first chapter—"the tendency to classify many of the great artists and thinkers of past ages as secret adherents of one's own philosophy."

Jerardine, her lover, asks: "Why do you find it necessary?"

Aliciane answers that for every "hard-faced, harsh-voiced, trousered woman cab driver, and indeed every stomach-turning transvestite everywhere, it helps to remember—" and she'd say two or three of the proud, disputed names.

The scorn with which the average Lesbian views her transvestite sister is manifold.

One Lesbian told me: "They're really sick. I don't even think of them as homosexuals. The only women who are attracted to them are cheap whores!"

Another said: "They spoil everything! My mother knows about me, but to her mind I'm associated with those dykes she sees strutting around in men's suits. I guess all the world thinks that's what a Lesbian is—one of those dykes!"

A third Lesbian I know, one who likes to drink in gay bars, told me: "Transvestites ruin gay bars. They bring in the bad element, the cheap chorus-girl type, and they attract attention to the bar by their dress. They can turn a nice quiet gay bar into a roaring commercial dive—a tourist attraction."

The Morgans and the Mikis and the Fortunes of the gay city are definitely considered to be the low-life element of metropolitan Lesbian life. The dykes half wear male clothing. Some go all the way—buying suits, shoes, ties, underwear etc., in men's stores. Others wear just the men's slacks and shirts. But all adopt, or have long since acquired, masculine mannerisms. They abstain from the use of cosmetics except for aftershave lotion, or hair tonic. If nature has been cruel enough to make their breasts full, they often bind their breasts to hide this "disfiguration." Male jewelry is a fetish with them—keychains, rings, watches, cuff links, tie clasps, and cigarette cases, are all cherished possessions. The dyke hates to be reminded that she is a woman.

Morgan, Fortune's friend from Atlantic City, said this to me: "I want to feel as much like a man as it's humanly possible. I'd feel freaky making love to a girl if I were wearing a dress. Those Lesbians who run around wearing dresses and making love to each other remind me of a bunch of schoolgirls with crushes."

Miki, her lover, a very feminine girl agreed: "If a woman in a dress were to approach me, I'd laugh in her face. I'd feel ridiculous going along the street arm in arm with someone wearing a dress! It's just creepy!"

The feminine half of the transvestite relationship was described this way, by "a member of a college faculty . . . who has had contact with all sorts of persons, including Lesbians" in Dr. George W. Henry's *All the Sexes*:

> "It isn't easy to spot a bitch—by her definition 'a helpless, passive femme'—on the street, in a café, or in your office. They're quite feminine in appearance, dress frilly, use make-up, and have feminine, even babyish voices."

The woman goes on to say that these "bitches" attract a certain type of gay girl who is "just dying to be leaned on." She refers to these "bitches" as "sweet leeches."

By inference, she suggests that in the transvestite relationship, the dyke is strong and dependable, a leaning post; someone to whom the feminine Lesbian can attach herself for moral, physical and financial support.

Miki's response to this was:

"Nothing can be farther from the truth! Dykes are the biggest babies in the world. When Morgan cuts her finger she carries on as if she'd severed a vein. When she gets her period you'd think she was in an advanced stage of cancer to hear her moaning over the cramps. I have to make all the decisions, and as far as finances go—just take a look at Morgan and figure out for yourself how limited her job opportunities are. In a horizontal position she's a lion, but, honey, vertically she's a little scared lamb. That's what flips me so much about her! She loves to play the great big man role—pick out my clothes, criticize my make-up, open doors for me, and be the one who asks for the check in a restaurant—but I know my baby. She needs me more than I need her."

Sara Harris, writing about prostitutes in *Cast The First Stone*, mentions the inordinate pride the whore takes in supporting her pimp. Pimps can be rough, cruel, mercenary, and unfaithful, she tells us, but, incredulously, the prostitute is proud that she can still support him. The prostitute seems to be saying: "I'm still able to keep my man. He still needs me to support his penchant for the track, liquor, clothes, and a car."

In the femme-dyke relationship there seems to be a parallel.

A friend of Miki's, a femme like Miki, who works as a hatcheck girl in a club in the West Forties told me: "The dyke I was going with left me when I was between jobs. It was a dirty thing to do. I'd supported her for six months. All she cared about was showing up every night in the bars with enough for a few drinks. She used to sleep all day and watch television; then around ten o'clock she'd head for the bars. I suppose she's still in them, and probably some other fool like myself is paying for it. I loved that kid and understood her. I just hope who ever has her now does."

Often it is only the genuine transvestite who is supported by the femme; by genuine transvestite I mean one who does not own any women's clothing, but "passes" completely as a man.

Arlene, or Allan, as she calls herself, is one of these. Occasionally she finds employment in a gay bar or nightclub or in a factory. She seldom holds a job very long. The reason for this is striped half with laziness, half with the inevitable embarrassment rising out of the fact that she looks every inch a man, but is every inch a woman. One of the main ways she is discovered develops in the unavoidable problem of having to use the bathroom in a public place. Then she is literally in a no man's land.

"As far as I'm concerned," Allan says, "I'm a man. I've taken out girls who don't even know I'm not. I've made love to them and they still don't know. But sometimes I get nervous. I'm always afraid some wise guy will spot me and try to start a fight. And when I'm out with a girl, unless I take her to a gay club, there's no place to go to the john."

While it seems incredible that a girl would not know another girl was making love to her, and not a man, history has recorded many such cases.

Havelock Ellis recorded several. In 1906 there was the case of the confidential secretary to the Russian Consul, a Mr. Nicholai de Raylan, who was married twice in the United States. The first wife received her divorce on grounds of cruelty and misconduct with chorus girls. The second wife, a widow with a child, was very devoted to her "husband." Neither wife ever suspected the truth, that their "husband" was a

woman, a fact that was learned at "his" death. Both women
ridiculed the idea that "he" could be a she. De Raylan, Ellis
tells us, wore a very elaborate constructed artificial penis.

Dr. Frank S. Caprio, writing in *Female Homosexuality*,
states that in Spain and Russia Lesbians have been known to
pass as men, and were accepted for military service. "It was
only upon their death," Caprio writes, "that their true identity
became known."

Arlene's—or Allan's—fear of "the wise guys who want to
start a fight" is one of her more realistic ideas. In Greenwich
Village there are often bands of young hoodlums who enjoy
picking on a transvestite, once they spot her. One night on 4th
Street I witnessed one such incident.

Ricky, a very masculine-looking transvestite, emerged
from a bar with a femme. Swaggering slightly from the beers
she'd downed, dressed in a man's suit, shirt, and tie, she was
arguing with the femme over the fact a man at the bar was too
attentive to the femme.

There was a small knot of young men standing outside
the bar observing this.

One said to Ricky: "Maybe the lady don't like your type."

"You keep out of this!" Ricky shouted at him.

"I *like* the lady," another said, "And I don't like your type."

Ricky tried to steer the femme down the street and away
from them, but they began to tag along after the pair.

"What can that dyke do to keep you happy?" one wanted
to know.

Another: "Hey, miss, where do you buy your ties? That
one's sharp, all right! Isn't it sharp, fellows?"

"Yeah, it sure is sharp! It's real groovy! You're a pretty
groovy dresser, miss!"

By this time, the femme was angry. "Make them go
away!" she told Ricky.

Ricky said: "What can *I* do?," but nonetheless, she tried.

Turning, she faced them: "Look, fellows, are *we* bothering *you*? Why don't you leave us alone?"

"Why should we? We like natty dressers like yourself!"

"Sure, we want to know where you buy your clothes!"

"And where you get good-looking dames like the lady!"

Then Ricky lost her temper: "I'm going to call the cops on you guys!" she shouted.

This set off a roar of laughter and catcalls.

"You big dyke!" one shouted. "Don't you know you're against the law!"

"Go on and call the cops!" another shouted.

And a third: "Why don't you fight like a man, if you want to act like one!" With that, he grabbed Ricky's coat.

Wildly, Ricky swung . . . and the fight was on.

The femme stood by squealing with horror while the young men punched Ricky, tossed her to the street, kicked at her and swore angrily. Through it all, Ricky could be heard crying out: "I'm a woman, you lousy bastards! I'm a woman!"

When the fight was finally broken up, Ricky was guided away from the scene by her femme. Ricky was holding a handkerchief to her bleeding face. Her suit was ripped, the shirt torn, the tie gone. Ricky was sobbing and the femme was saying: "Dirty rotten men! They're all that way! And they wonder why we hate them!"

"I never saw anything like that!" someone standing beside me in the crowd said.

His companion answered: "I did. In fact I saw something even funnier. I saw one of them bull-dykes once who was pregnant!"

Some genuine transvestites are so insistent on being the male, that they cannot stand to have their bodies touched during love-making. A transvestite studied by Dr. George W. Henry in his book *Sex Variants*, who told him "I don't like to say I'm supporting a woman. I would rather have her take care of me," also told him she did not mind if a woman "went down" (performed cunnilingus) on her, but she could not stand to be touched on her body. She was quoted:

"While a woman is going down on me, I visualize myself as a man and I talk as if I were a man. I say 'Isn't that good? Oh, baby, isn't that good!'"

But let a woman touch her breasts, or elsewhere, and her passion goes.

There are transvestites who never allow their femmes to see them naked. Many of them always wear pajamas to bed, and lock the bathroom door while they are bathing or dressing.

A femme told me: "My girl hates any mention of the fact she is menstruating. I have to buy the Kotex and keep it in the hall closet—she'd rather die than buy a box of it. If I say anything to her about the curse, she flys into a rage. I pretend I don't know when she has it."

What is it that attracts these femmes to transvestites?

"Dykes are sweeter and more gentle than a man," some tell you.

Others say: "A dyke looks just like a man, but is a hundred times better as a lover. A dyke knows how to love a woman, because she wants very little from sex for herself. She just wants to please the woman. A man is a brute. He just wants a woman for his own pleasure."

Morgan's Miki told me: "My analyst told me I'm not really homosexual; I'm bisexual. He said women who are attracted to the pseudo-male Lesbian prove that they are lured by what is masculine. That's right. I think I'd like men if they'd stop trying to prove their virility, if they'd act a little more dependent and a little more sentimental. I like to feel needed—not just as a cook and someone to go to bed with, but as a friend. I have that with Morgan. I've never had it with a man."

These answers are invariably glib and oversimplified. Too

many homosexuals blame the male nature for the fact that they are abnormal. She who does not desire to be conquered by the male, or possessed by him, criticizes that very proclivity in him for aggressiveness and physical domination which the normal female submits to gratefully and lovingly.

The femme who is attracted to the transvestite often is simply a carbon copy of the kind of woman she would be if she were a heterosexual. Many femmes work as hostesses in nightclubs, as B-girls, as whores. In some instances if they were normal, they would look for the same kind of man they now have in a transvestite—a man they could "keep." He might be a wonderful, gentle lover; and ostensibly, a great sentimental-ist, but like the "little boy" a lot of transvestites are, he proba-bly won't be able to hold a job long, probably won't be able to bear a cut on his finger, and probably will need the girl more than she needs him.

To better illustrate this, one femme I know who spoke of man's brutality to women was pushed down a flight of stairs by her transvestite girl friend. Her broken ankle in a cast, she told me: "Blackie didn't really mean to hurt me. It was just one of those things. She lost her temper suddenly."

By the same token, there are countless women, who when beaten by their men, offer the same sort of rationalization.

Man's inhumanity to women probably has very little to do with the femmes' choice of a Lesbian partner. A dyke is often afraid to use her fists in an encounter with a man, but many femmes have been on the receiving end of those fists.

Fortune, the girl who came out in Atlantic City, falls into a slightly different category of transvestite. Her kind usually work, and is usually not afraid to brave the world in heels and hose when it is absolutely necessary. Her girls, while feminine in appearance, are usually not the breadwinners. More often these pairs "go dutch," splitting the bills between them.

The majority of transvestites in New York City live in or

around Greenwich Village. There they attract less attention on the streets and in the stores and restaurants.

One transvestite told me: "I haven't been above Fourteenth Street in six years. I like it down here. I belong here—it's my home. The Village is my home."

In the next chapter we will meet another clique of Village Lesbians, who call the Village "home." Between the two groups there is little friendliness. About the second clique a femme told me: "They really hand me a laugh, running around like they was still going to college. They all look alike. You can't tell the dyke from the lady; they're like two peas in a pod. They're queer queers, if you ask me."

"Why can't a woman be more like a man!" I smiled.

The femme said emphatically: "Exactly!"

4. THE CIRCLE IN THE SQUARE

It is a small dinner party on West 4th Street, off Washington Square in Greenwich Village. The occasion is the first-year anniversary of Jacqueline Spencer and Connie Keene. The year is reckoned not by the day they met each other, but the day they began living together.

It is eight o'clock. Cynthia Fullerton, the girl who "brought Jackie out," is there with Selma, her present girl friend. They have been going together for only two or three months, and do not yet live in the same apartment. Sitting side by side on the studio couch, Cynthia and Selma are very affectionate with each other, their hands meeting now and then; their eyes, often. They seem to share some desperate secret.

Jackie and Connie can remember when they were in that stage. They know that once the pair settle down together, they will simmer down as well; but seeing them in this tender condition is touching and nostalgic. Both Jackie and Connie recall when they felt that way about one another, and about others. Indeed, Jackie and Cynthia felt that way once.

The foursome is waiting for Doris and Lou, another couple who live over on Jones Street.

The apartment is a four-floor walk-up "railroad" with a fireplace. Jackie and Connie have made it "interesting." An

exposed steam pipe in one corner is painted orange. The walls
are white. Foreign travel posters hang on the walls. The two
studio couches have dark green burlap covers to match the
burlap drapes. There are two sling chairs by the homemade
marble-topped coffee table. The plain wood floor is painted
dark brown, spattered with beige and black dots, with two
straw scatter rugs tossed across it. In the bookcase are many of
Jackie's old college textbooks and a small pocketbook collection of Lesbian novels: *The Price of Salt*, *Spring Fire*, *Queer
Patterns*, *Odd Girl Out*, and *Women's Barracks*.

All four girls wear pants—chinos, frontier pants, or
bermuda shorts with knee-length socks. This is the standard
uniform for "the circle in the square" during leisure hours,
unless they are attending theater, eating dinner in one of the
better restaurants, or entertaining friends from the office,
brothers, friends from back home, or—day of panic—mothers and fathers.

It is winter. Cynthia and Selma have hung their short,
warm car coats in the hall. These coats are part of the uniform
too. Usually they have large pockets and are fastened by
leather or cloth cords which loop around leather or wooden
barrel-shaped buttons.

The girls wear shirts or heavy, bulky woolen sweaters—
sometimes turtle-necks. Like as not, around their necks they
wear leather cords, or chains, which hold various charms.

They are on their first round of Martinis. The conversation began when Jackie remarked that she believed the girl
who moved in across the hall is gay. She looked gay—always
wore chinos and a car coat—and the boy who helped her
move in, Jackie said, "is a faggot I've seen around for ages."

The discussion is now centered on male homosexuals.

"You can't depend on them," Cynthia Fullerton is saying;
"I know. When I was married to Tony I could never rely on
him for any kind of appointment we might have together.

If something came up—another man, for instance—he just didn't show up."

Jackie says: "Well he couldn't depend on you, either. After all, you kicked him out when we started going together."

"We'd had it by then," Cynthia shrugs. "He ran off on me in Mexico City once—just left me flat, to go with some pasty-faced old fag harpsichordist."

"You'd have done the same," Jackie insists.

Selma intervenes on Cynthia's behalf: "I know what Cynthia means. Faggots don't want to settle down with anyone. Look at the way they run from bar to bar night after night. Always on the prowl. They don't look for love—they look for sex!"

Connie laughs. "Hey, Jackie, remember that fag we met at The Dock the other night! This is funny. Listen, Jackie and I were in The Dock having a drink, and we got into conversation with this gay boy. We were telling him that we were going to celebrate our anniversary soon, and he insisted on buying us a drink. I could die when I think about it—listen. He said he'd like to settle down but he'd been involved once and it had nearly killed him."

Jackie interrupts: "He didn't use the word 'involved.' He said he'd had a serious affair once, with a man he'd met in a bar. He said they both fell madly in love with one another, and couldn't be out of each other's sight."

"Yes," Connie continues, "that's it. He said he'd never felt that way before about anyone. He said it was beautiful—that they just idolized each other. He said he could never stand to go through anything like that again, because when they finally broke up, it just threw him into shock."

"We were very sympathetic," Jackie takes over, "and we told him that one day he'd find someone else and settle down again. But he kept protesting he couldn't go through that a second time."

Connie says: "So I asked him how long he'd gone with the man. You know what he said? He said: two weeks!"

The four burst into laughter.

"Two weeks!" Connie repeats. "That's their idea of a serious affair!"

Cynthia Fullerton exclaims: "*Tell* me! Tony went home with this man once, and the man stopped at the corner on the way and bought a toothbrush for Tony. The next morning when Tony went into his bathroom to wash up, he saw a whole wall with toothbrushes hanging on it. The guy kept track that way."

"I wouldn't be able to stand it if I were a man," Selma says. "They go home with anyone. Sometimes they don't even exchange names. It's so cold!"

"It's dirty somehow," Connie says. "I think it's repulsive. I know some of them aren't that way—but most of them are."

"Oh, they *all* are, basically!" Cynthia answers. She takes Selma's hand. "If you ever looked at someone else, I'd want to kill you—and her."

"Don't worry, honey," Selma tells her, "I'm not looking."

"Faggots have no real emotions," Jackie declares. "They're just sex machines. Thank God we're not that bad, anyway!"

Then Doris and Lou arrive. And for the rest of this evening anyway, the male homosexuals are off the spit. Another round of Martinis is served and the subject changes to Lou's mother.

"When will she be here?" Cynthia asks.

"Tomorrow night. I've got Art Edwards—remember him, he does the windows for Johnson's Department Store, goes around with that decorator crowd? I've got him to take us to dinner. He'll be the 'boy friend.'"

Lou smiles at Doris. She is an apprentice to a silversmith in the Village. Doris works for a magazine uptown. Both are in their early twenties. They've been together a year and a half.

Doris says, "All I hope is that your mother doesn't dig Art. Good God, he's a real screaming swish."

"Mother will just think he's a very nice, polite boy."

"Does she suspect about you at all?" Selma asks.

"I honestly don't *think* so. It used to worry her because in high school I had crushes on other girls. At the time she used to be sort of embarrassed about it. I think she's just pushed it as far back in her consciousness as she can."

"Selma's mother is the prize," Cynthia says. "She's so bitter about her own marriage she just prays God Selma won't ever take the leap. Homosexuality never occurs to her! She just keeps saying, 'Don't get married—you're too young to get in that mess.'"

Connie laughs. "My father's that way. A few years ago I thought I might marry this fellow. I was awfully unhappy at the time. I'd had this miserable affair with Jane Birkett. I thought I'd just duck out on the gay life. When I told my dad I was considering marriage, he said 'Connie, you're only thirty-one! You're too young to tie yourself down!' He'll be saying that when I'm forty-two."

Jackie says: "My dad's more tolerant. He'd love to see me happy, and settled down with a man. He'd adore to have me married to a man . . . just as long as he was a man."

Connie serves another round of Martinis.

Selma says: "Lou, your mother's coming to town reminds me of a poem I heard once, about two gay girls in the same situation." Selma recites:

Raise your voice an octave,
Wear a skirt around,
Mother doesn't get the bit
And she'll be in town.

Call some faggots, darling,
Ask them by for drinks,

Mother's on her way, my love,
And I'm straight, she thinks.

Push our beds apart, pet,
Put our rings away,
Mother doesn't understand,
She arrives today.

By now, everyone is a little high. Cynthia and Selma, Doris and Lou, toast Jackie and Connie. The conversation ranges from a discussion of their individual jobs—Jackie is still with the airlines and still trying to write a book; Connie, like Cynthia, is a photographer, and Selma is a medical secretary—to television, to who goes with whom, to parents. Jackie keeps mentioning the fact that she thinks the girl across the hall is gay.

While they roast hot dogs and hamburgers over charcoal in the fireplace, Connie snaps at Jackie: "If you're so interested in the girl across the hall, go across the hall."

Jackie says: "I just think the poor kid's gay, and might like to meet some others."

"You think everyone's gay!" Connie says.

"Well, I'll bet ten dollars she is!"

"Have her over," Lou says. "Ask her if she wants to come over for a drink."

Doris says: "Is she home?"

"Sure. I can hear her radio going over there."

Connie glares at Jackie. "Cruising on our anniversary," she says. "That's just swell!"

After coffee there is a temporary lull. No one is ready yet for another drink. They watch television for a while. Lou suggests going to the bars later, and Connie drags Cynthia back to the darkroom to show her some of her new equipment.

Time passes.

Charades? No one feels up to it.

Poker? Too broke.

Bridge? Lou doesn't play.

Jackie opens a quart of beer, and again mentions the girl across the hall.

"All right!" Connie sighs. "Let's ask her over for a drink. Maybe we need a new face."

"I'm not going to do it if you're going to be mad, Con."

"Jackie, I'm not *mad*! I just don't see why you care whether or not the girl across the hall is gay!"

"Oh, Con," Lou says, "don't be so jealous! It'd be fun to meet someone new."

"We don't even know if she *is* gay," Connie says.

Jackie says flatly. "She *is*, don't worry!"

More time passes; more beer is passed around. Then finally Jackie announces that she is going across the hall and ask the girl over.

While she is gone, Connie broods. Lou mentions a second time that it might be fun to go to the bars later. "After all," she says to Doris, "Mother's going to be here for two weeks. We won't be able to go anyplace."

"You won't," says Doris.

"Would you go to The Dock without me?"

"Well, what am I supposed to do while you chase around town with your mother and a faggot?"

Now *Lou* broods.

The Dock is the accepted hangout for the circle in the square. Often, after drinking at The Dock, they progress to more honkytonk spots where Lesbians cavort, but The Dock is the springboard. Some members of the circle in the square will not go even to The Dock. They either do not have the money to spend in bars, do not drink very much, if at all, or simply prefer to mingle with their own kind at home, or in the homes of other Lesbians.

The majority, however, visit the bars at least one night every two weeks. Many, once or twice a night every week. Usually couples make dates to meet other couples there; seldom does one girl from this clique go alone, as Doris has suggested she will.

Now, Jackie returns, smiling with satisfaction.

"She's coming over," she says.

"What did she say?"

"Not too much. I don't think she was dressed. It took her a while to answer my knock, and then she didn't open the door. I explained that we were neighbors, and we'd like to have her over for a drink. She said she'd be over in about ten minutes."

"Satisfied now?" Connie says.

"Aw, come on, Con. I don't mean anything like you think."

Connie says: "Happy anniversary! Aren't we having fun!"

They have another round of drinks. Doris and Lou aren't speaking to each other. Cynthia and Selma, their bond made more intense by the tensions around them, are holding hands and looking at one another with a we-aren't-like-them expression. Jackie is pouring more beer into everyone's glasses.

When the knock comes at the door, Jackie answers.

In the doorway stands the girl across the hall. Her hair is worn gamine-style. She has on washed-out jeans, a man's white shirt, and soiled white sneakers. Her eyes seem sleep-swollen and unaccustomed to the light.

She says to Jackie: "Hi! Mind if I bring my friend too?"

"Gosh, no!" Jackie says. "Bring her!"

The girl smiles. "It's a him." She reaches out her hand, and a tall young man slips up beside her. His hair is matted from sleep; his eyes too, blink in the bright light.

"We're a little drowsy," the young man says as he enters the room, his arm around the girl's waist.

"This is Bill," the girl says to everyone. "I'm Nancy. I don't know whether we're in very good condition to meet our neighbors."

They look deeply into one another's eyes and chuckle.

Connie says in an ironic tone, looking across at Jackie with a tip to her lips: "I don't know that we're in condition to meet our neighbors either, but pull up a beer, and welcome."

A half an hour later, after Bill and Nancy have gone back across the hall, Connie says: "That was just great! Did you see him take us in?"

"He didn't say two words." Doris laughs. "God, wasn't that embarrassing!"

"I don't think either one noticed anything," Jackie says.

Connie laughs: "Are you kidding? A bunch of girls all sitting around on a Saturday night together, in pants, getting fried. He got the bit, honey, don't worry."

"Sure, he did," Lou says. "She did too. Remember the way she said, 'Do you two live together?' to you, Con."

"*Tell* me," Connie sighs.

"He kept looking at your ring, Connie."

"I know. I know. It was just *swell*! I love to have the neighbors know the score."

"Let's go to The Dock," Lou says.

Jackie murmurs. "So I made a mistake!"

"Want to go The Dock?" Lou asks again.

"No," Doris answers. "Let's wait for your mother to arrive and take her."

Lou shouts: "Look, Doris, it isn't my fault that my mother's going to visit us! Did I ask her? What do you want me to do, tell her she can't come? You make me so damn mad!"

"Don't shout, Lou, please! Our neighbors know enough about us already." Connie stands up and stretches. "Maybe we ought to go on over to The Dock. The walk will clear our heads."

"Yes, let's go!" Selma agrees. She presses Cynthia's hand gently. "Want to, honey?"

"If you want to."

"We won't stay long. Just for one drink. Want to?"

"Sure," Cynthia says. "Okay, doll."

It is nearing midnight, and snowing outside in the streets. Through Washington Square Park three pairs of girls pass. The pair in the lead walk briskly, their hands stuffed into the pockets of their car coats, their collars turned up against the weather.

"I still don't think they noticed anything," one is protesting. "Why make something out of nothing, honey?"

The pair in the middle ignore one another in an unhappy silence. The snow scrunches beneath their desert boots.

Behind them, Cynthia and Selma walk, touching.

"We'll never fight the way they do, will we?" Selma asks.

Soon, these members of the circle in the square will arrive at The Dock. We will join them there later.

Meanwhile, let's get a cab and head uptown.

5. THE GIRL IN THE BROOKS BROTHERS SHIRT

Jane Allen, a copywriter for a large advertising agency, came up the hard way. For years she managed to live on one of those unlivable salaries prestige jobs pay. In the agency where she is still employed, she began her career typing, filing, taking dictation, pasting news clips in the publicity department's scrap book, and sorting television mail. She worked overtime, brought work home at night, and during her lunch hour attended agency-sponsored lectures on the various phases of advertising.

"I was a long time getting where I am," she said. "I went from twenty-six hundred to nine thousand in six years' time, and I'm not at the top yet."

Jane used to live on Waverly Place in Greenwich Village. If she came up the hard way, she also "came out" the hard way. She had a series of miserable affairs with girls who were not her equal socially, economically, or intellectually.

"I landed in the Village right out of college. When I got in with the gay crowd down there, I went all out. I began to dress in the village uniform, talk the gay lingo, haunt the bars on weekends, and have long intense sessions with ex–boy friends during which I somehow always felt obliged to confess to them that I was a Lesbian. I soared to the heights and sank to the depth so many times I felt like a stunt pilot's barometer. I was in and out of love, and in and out of bed. I knew the words to every torch song going. I was a Jew in the Promised Land. In college I'd been straight, but I always felt this immense attraction to other girls. In college I was very particular about the man I dated. He had to be intelligent, well-mannered, and ambitious. When I got to the Village and started going with girls, it didn't matter—so long as they were girls. I wasn't realistic about anything but my work, and my work saved me. Thank God I had to make a living, otherwise I might be down in the Village acting like an idiot!"

Through another girl in Jane's agency, Jane met some uptown Lesbians. About the same time, she was promoted.

"Then I began to see the light," Jane told me. "Suddenly I was embarrassed to be in with the Village crowd. I was tired of being a 'card-carrying Lesbian.' I wanted to be more chic. I didn't want the whole world to know what I was. Why should they? I began to worry that I might run into people from the agency on the street, in the Village, when I was running around in Chinos with another Lesbian. After all, I was working on three major accounts—a soap, baby-food, and spaghetti. I had to be more careful, and I wanted to be. I wasn't getting any younger. I decided to move uptown."

What happened to Jane happens to many gay girls who begin in the Village. A career often prompts the move. Age has something to do with it, too.

Jane said: "When you're twenty-two or twenty-three it might be all right to run around in pants down in Greenwich Village with the other Bohemians. But when you're thirty and holding down a responsible job, it's ludicrous! Sometimes a bunch of us from uptown eat down there, and occasionally we go slumming in the bars for a ball, but I'd never live there again. Never!"

A male homosexual I know, a rather glib young artist,

who knows many gay girls, had this to say—stated in his particular vernacular:

> Lesbians are really evil, particularly in their middle-thirties, when they're launched on their careers. They ruin their lives! The downtown clique decide to brave it uptown in heels and hose thinking no one could tell what they were. They all buy poodles and get unlisted phones. They drink less and save their money, and their affairs last for years! It's so evil! They never have any fun—just worry about their seams being straight, and the motors in their Volkswagons holding out. And of course, those who are already uptown can't abide the invasion, so they move out of town to the country, swarming all over the meadows and hills, buying up old windmills and converting them into houses. Evil, evil! They even take out insurance together, the good Lord pity them!

Not all of the uptown clique are as affluent as Jane; not all hold down good jobs that involve as much responsibility as Jane's, nor carry as much prestige. Jane's girl friend, Deenie, is an example. Deenie is a secretary to a magazine editor. She makes less than sixty-five dollars a week take-home pay. She is Jane's age, thirty-two, but she is not quite Jane's equal in education and ability. Therefore, Jane carries the bulk of their expenses. It is Jane's Hillman Mynx; Jane's furniture in the apartment on East 93rd Street; Jane's charge accounts which both use to purchase their clothes; and Jane's salary which both draw on for summer vacations in East Hampton, and a side trip in mid-winter to Nassau.

The uptown gay girls are often divided into Janes and Deenies, with one carrying the load for both. In some instances, a "Jane" will carry the whole load, with only an occasional "token" payment now and then from her girl friend. Many uptown Lesbians, like Jane, are in their middle thirties; and like Jane too, many have had a vast amount of affairs. For them, when they are between affairs, the "new face" is at a premium. She may be a divorcée who has just gone gay, a young girl from the office who was just brought out, or a new girl in town. Whoever she is, she is the belle of the ball. And quite commonly, she is courted in an elaborate manner—taken to dinner, to the theater, to the country, etc. When she is conquered, she is supported, for the most part, by her Caesar.

Huguette, the young French girl, is an example. No longer a resident in the Evangeline Home, Huguette lives with Tay, and works for her still—at an increase in salary.

To the uptown gay girl, being chic is paramount. The foreign car, the unlisted phone, the poodle, and the East Side address are essential. The Hamptons is a must for summer vacations, with a side trip to Cherry Grove, on Fire Island. It is assumed that an uptown gay girl has been to Europe at least once; and to all important shows during the theater season. Parties are often catered affairs; Sunday brunches and intimate dinner gatherings are a regular part of the routine.

Quite common to the uptown clique, too, are the couples who cannot really afford the necessities involved in "belonging." They buy on time, and go into debt to maintain the standards. One girl I know put it this way:

"Kathy and I only make about a hundred and fifty a week between us. We're in hock up to our necks, and we can't save a dime. Sometimes it depresses us, but we figure that we're no worse off than any heterosexual couple in a similar situation. If you want nice friends, you can't be always living on the fringe of their lives. You have to be a part of their lives. The lucky ones with the money set the pace, and we have to keep up with it. It's the same in business. Certain things are expected of you, that's all. A decent address, nice clothes, and money to spend for entertainment.".

Kathy and her girl are one of the few couples who share all expenses equally.

Poker parties among the girls uptown are a popular form of entertainment.

"We've lost ten and fifteen dollars some nights," Kathy's friend said, "and we really don't have it to lose. But you can't keep turning down invitations. Sometimes, of course, we win, and it evens out, but there are nights when I dread the telephone call asking us over for a game of poker."

One of the reasons poker parties are so popular uptown, is that much of the entertainment among the gay girls in that crowd is at home. When ten or twelve of them get together, poker seems a logical diversion, rather than going out where they might be conspicuous by their number.

Sometimes, however, there is an occasion to go out. Let's go along with a group to an art exhibit.

The gallery is on West 57th Street. It has been hired by Olivia, a stage manager, for her girl friend's showing. Tanja has been painting for three or four years, ever since she moved in with Olivia and gave up her job as a salesgirl to undergo analysis. Brochures and formal announcements were sent out by Olivia a few weeks before. Olivia is one of the social lionesses of the uptown crowd. She is rich, handsome, and very successful. Few of the girls will want to miss Tanja's opening.

When we arrive, we find a small crowd already milling about in the two rooms that contain the exhibit. Most of them are women. A slender, pale-faced young man who combs his hair forward and clips it across his forehead in a short-bangs effect, beckons us over to the champagne table. There, he is busy popping corks and pouring the drink into glasses rented for the occasion.

"Do you know who's here?" he whispers. He says the name of a Broadway actress whose show Olivia worked with. "She's over there," he confides. "She's got heavy glasses on, if you don't recognize her right away. I think it's divine that she came. Tanja's in another world, of course, the darling! Olivia's just broken her back over this whole affair."

He is Roger, a male homosexual who scurries around on the fringes of Olivia's life. An aspiring actor who has not been very successful and who is trying desperately not to age, Roger often acts as an escort for Olivia and Tanja in public.

We see Tay and Huguette standing in a corner, and we join them.

Huguette is admiring a painting of the Eiffel Tower. It was done last summer while Olivia and Tanja were in Paris.

"It's not good at all," Tay comments. "It's like everything the child tries to do. Too commercial. Too much like an illustration. I feel sorry for Olivia. She tries so hard for that kid, and the kid just doesn't have it!"

Huguette says: "You are too critical, Tay. Really!"

"Honey, I just happen to know a little about art, that's all."

We remember meeting Huguette shortly after she moved in with Tay. Was she happy?

"Happy?" she said, "No, not especially. But I'm cheerful."

And how did she feel about Tay?

"I am dominated, and I am spoiled. She is like my father. She is stern, and generous. I respect her so much, and fear her very much. She told me I should forget about men if I am with her. I think I have. I never had too much experience with them anyway. But I wonder if after we break up I will want a man. I don't know. I sometimes look at other women on the street with men, and I feel sad for myself. But that is it."

We asked her what made her sad.

"In France I was a straight Catholic. It was my upbringing. I think sometimes I should have children, and worry that

I never will. I think I should be making a house for a man, and worry that I never will. But no man I have met has been like Tay to me except my father. I wish women could have children together. I think I would never be unhappy then."

Then we say hello to Tanja.

"Did you see who's here?" she asks us, naming the Broadway actress Roger pointed out to us earlier.

"My analyst wouldn't come," she continues. "It depressed me awfully, but Olivia says they won't ever mix socially with their patients."

How is analysis coming, we ask?

"I'm progressing. I still have a lot of hostility, though."

Olivia steps up and says: "Who doesn't? We'll work it out, honey." She smiles at us. "Did you see who's here?"

We nod.

"Tay's down there making like an art critic," Olivia says. "I should have hired a bouncer. Look, Tanja, love," she turns to Tanja, "call up Janie Allen and Deenie and tell them not to bring their car. If we're all going out together after, we might as well take ours. Their private number's in my book, in my purse. Try to catch them before they leave, all right, sweet?"

Tanja leaves, and Olivia says to us:

"Poor kid overheard Tay sounding off and threw her for a loop. That's all she needs at this point. She's always had a complex anyway about not being able to do anything creative, and that goddam doctor's planted the idea in her head that she's a masochist. I'm going to call him up and ask him what the hell I'm paying him for, anyway! Tay can just drag her behind out of here and take that Huguette with her. You kids doing anything later? We thought we might get a kick out of eating in the Village and dropping in on some of the bars. Haven't done it in years and year! Want to meet us?"

We agree, and Olivia waves to a couple entering the gallery.

"Berry and Billie," she says. "God, I think Berry's crocked!" Berry is a television writer; her girl, Billie, is a social secretary. Both are slightly high. Even without the stimulus of liquor, Berry is always a trifle loud. She wears a charcoal-gray suit with a mink collar, carries a cigarette attached to an ivory holder, and enters crying: "Can I double-park outside, Olivia? We can't stay! We're on our way to the vets and we've got Miss McCullers and Roughneck with us. We didn't want to drag them in!"

Billie says: "They're disgraceful, anyway. They need to be clipped!"

"We just left Michael's Pub," Berry shouts. "Jane Allen and Deenie are over there. They're on their way!"

"God," Billie sighs, "I can't drink any more! But I'm dying to see Tanja's stuff. How much is this one, Olivia? The one of the Eiffel Tower?"

Olivia murmurs to us: "For God's sake, don't they know enough to go up to Roger and ask the price discreetly. They're turning it into a goddam auction! Excuse me, I've got to catch Tanja and tell her Janie and Deenie are at Michael's Pub."

Behind us we hear Tay telling Huguette: "I'm not criticizing your taste in art. That would be impossible. You don't have any."

Huguette is following after her, fighting back tears.

We have another glass of champagne.

"I think it's going over grand," Roger tell us. "Did you see who was here? She just left. I hope it's going over all right. Olivia's knocked herself out to give the kid a big sendoff. Olivia's one in a million. She's hung by her toes on that kid!"

More couples arrive. Judy and Grace, and two illustrators. Judy used to go with Olivia; Grace with Jane Allen's Deenie. Both of them, at one time, went with Berry.

Judy is A.A. She tried to drown herself one drunken night at Cherry Grove on Fire Island when Olivia announced she was through. She was rescued by the cab driver who runs the jeep between there and Ocean Beach on the island. Grace, who was not "attached" at the time, had a long talk with her the next day, and their summer romance was launched.

We hear Olivia say: "Hi, doll. Judy, you look marvelous! Want some—oops, no you don't want any champagne, do you!"

Grace smiles at Judy. "It's been seven months now."

"You kids been together seven months?" Olivia exclaims.

"No," Grace says, "I mean since Judy had a drink."

Olivia says, "I'm proud of you, baby. Real proud of you!"

"Thanks, Olly," Judy says. "And I'm proud of Tanja. Her work looks great. No kidding!"

"Tell her that, doll! She needs a little encouragement. That goddam analyst she's going to has her thinking she's a goddam masochist or something. I don't know what I'm paying him for!"

Now, Berry and Billie are leaving, shouting good-bys:

"Sorry we can't hang around," Berry says, "worried about the car! Miss McCullers is out there barking her lungs out! Listen, Olly, call us, huh? Let's get together, play poker or something!"

"Bye," Billy calls out. "We bought the Eiffel Tower. Just love it! Going to hang it over the fireplace by the Picasso etching! Loved her stuff, Olly! Good Lord, where is she? We didn't even say hello. Bye!"

"Bye!" Olivia says. "Call us and we'll get together."

"We're coming, Miss McCullers!" Berry shouts.

Gradually the crowd thins out.

"Did you see who was here?" we hear Roger saying, as he pops another cork.

"Then why did you bring me if I am so stupid on art?" Huguette passes with Tay.

"If he's really interested in me," Tanja tells Olivia, "He'd have come. Analyst or not!"

Olivia answers: "Well, damn it, honey, now you *are* talking like a masochist! Sweetie-lamb, analysts just don't mix socially."

"It's been seven months now," we hear Grace say to another couple. "I'm so proud of her."

"Janie!" Olivia calls out. "Deenie! Darlings!"

"We're double-parked," Janie says, "do you think it'll be all right, Olly?"

We leave the gallery finally, and stand out in front for a moment.

A Thunderbird starts with a roar, backing into the little red Volkswagon behind it. A Hillman Mynx is double-parked beside a Morris Minor. As we turn to walk down 57th Street, Huguette flees ahead of us, weeping. Then a Sunbeam Talbot squeals to a stop. The girl in the driver's seat asks: "Is the party over in there?"

"Not yet," we call back.

Tay passes us muttering: "As far as I'm concerned, the party's over!"

We think of a poem we heard once at a gay party:

I love the girl in the Brooks Brothers shirt,
She has pear conde and Martells for dessert,
She's gay as can be and off her noodle,
But she drives a Jag and she owns a poodle,
She's an uptown girl, she's smart, she's chic—
She'll leave me flat in about a week
But I love the girl in the Brooks Brothers shirt,
Though she has eyes for a gray flannel skirt.

6. THE VERY GAY, COME-WHAT-MAY PLACES

The Dock is on a side street, off Washington Square in New York's Greenwich Village. You could walk right by it without knowing it was there. There is no sign outside; there are no lights visible to the street. It is in the basement of a corner building, and save for the people going in and out, it does not look like a bar or restaurant. It's both.

The interesting thing about The Dock is that its clientele is not exclusively Lesbian, nor is it one of those Village spots whose admixture of Lesbians and men on the prowl makes it a commercial dive or a tourist bit.

Mac, the owner of The Dock, tries his best to run a nice place.

"I don't want servicemen in here," he says, "and I don't want wise guys in here. Those kind cause trouble. They bother the girls, and they start fights. On the other hand, the N.Y.U. boys come in here and act like gentlemen. Lots of times they bring dates. They don't bother the girls, and the girls don't bother them. The girls tell me I run the best place in town."

Mac's statement that he runs the best place in town for the gay girl to patronize is probably correct. It is one of the few gay bars for women that attempts to create atmosphere. It is a large long room candlelit—with knobby pine tables, fishnet strung along the walls, and a blazing fireplace in the rear. The jukebox offers a vast selection; the songs are the latest. Music is a must in a gay bar; the gay girl is almost always on the qui vive with the new recordings.

Tonight is a typical night in The Dock. Mac stands just inside the door, checking those who enter. No servicemen, no wise guys—and no one who is '86'—86 means unwanted trouble. For the most part, the people who come in The Dock are not turned away. This too is unusual.

Tonight at the bar there is a group of four girls, three men, a man and a woman, and at the end by the jukebox, a girl by herself. The four girls are regulars; they come in often for a few beers. They come in to gossip, to look around, to drink. They wear the gay uniform—chinos, a shirt—sometimes a wool sports sweater with a scarf at the neck. Three have characteristic short haircuts in various styles—gamine, feather cut, bob, feminine style; and one has long hair. All four are in their early twenties. They're discussing a movie they saw.

The three men are students from New York University. They've dropped in a few times after class. They like to look around and to watch the girls. One of them thinks the girls will all grow out of it. Another argues that once a girl is made love to by a Lesbian, she never wants a man again. A third just can't imagine what Lesbians do together. Sometimes the trio get into conversation with the girls, but they never try too hard. They know Mac doesn't like it when the girls complain about men bothering them.

The man and woman at the bar couldn't care less about those around them. They're in love; they're having a fight. The man thinks the woman is in with her boss. The woman says she is tired of waiting for the man's divorce to come through. The man has an apartment around the corner. He comes into The Dock for dinner three or four nights a week. Lesbians don't particularly interest him. The Dock just happens to be in his neighborhood.

The girl at the end of the bar is Kit. She is twenty-two, wants to be a playwright and works as a clerk-typist in a book publishing house. She also writes esoteric poetry. She is short, pretty and confused. Since she left the family manor in New Jersey two years ago and took her own apartment over on Bleeker Street, she has been in love seven times. She began by falling in love with a gay boy who introduced her to a gay crowd. The other six were women—rather, girls—like herself.

Kit is often in The Dock alone. She always carries a book she pretends to read, as she sips gin with bitters. Sometimes it is a copy of *The Little Princess* by Antoine de Saint-Exupéry, with passages heavily underlined: i.e.:

> *"One runs the risk of weeping a little, if one lets himself be tamed . . ."*

Sometimes it is a copy of *The Prophet* by Kahlil Gibran:

> *"All things shall love do unto you that you may know the secrets of your heart . . ."*

Or sometimes, *Fruits of the Earth*, by Gide:

> *"Love without caring whether what you love is good or bad . . ."*

Kit is usually "just over" an affair; usually, torching.

She does not want company. She reads and drinks, reads and drinks, with a melancholy expression on her face. Occasionally she stares off into space, or holds her head with her hands. When she is a little drunker, she plays the jukebox; plays a particular song over and over.

There are two types of torch songs among gay girls; two types of gay girls' "torches"—the proud and the pitiful. The proud torch assumes an "I'll never have anything like that again" attitude. The proud torch listens to such songs as "They Can't Take That Away From Me," "Just One Of Those Things." "I'll Remember April," and "Have A Good Time." The pitiful torch is not made of such stolid stuff; it is a drooping, weeping, self-pitying torch. The pitiful torch listens to such songs as "Where Are You?" "Not For Me," "It Never Entered My Mind," and "Guess Who I Saw Today."

Kit, along with the book, always carries a pitiful torch.

Tonight she is playing "Something To Live For" over and over; singing along with the words:

> . . . *oh what I wouldn't give for*
> *Someone to take my life and make it seem*
> *gay as they say it ought to be . . .*

Leaving the bar, wandering back among the tables, we see many groups of girls gathered at the tables. At a back table, there is a familiar group. Fresh from their walk through Washington Square, after dinner around the fireplace at Jackie and Connie's are those two, Doris and Lou—still on the subject of the impending visit from Lou's mother—and the new lovers, Selma and Cynthia. By now they are fairly drunk. They talk of what happened when the girl across the hall came over for the drink, of who is at The Dock, and of where to go next. Whenever the door slams at the entrance, they look up to see who has arrived.

It is hard to know what the gay girls expect from The Dock and places like it; hard to put your finger on what they look for. Some look for other girls, others simply look at other girls. When a group of couples are all together at a table, they look for something to talk about. And they sit, as though on review before the others.

You hear them say:

"Good God, look at that!" about the aging, lonely female in the black tailored suit, wandering about dismally by the bar—alone.

"She's a little tramp! She knows the color of everyone's sheets in town!" about Kit, the girl at the end of the bar.

"There's Liz Roy. Her father's a millionaire!" About a well-dressed woman at the next table, her fur coat hung cape-style around her shoulders; drinking Scotch on the rocks, in intimate conversation with a girl in a polo coat.

"Hey, look who Buzz Dutton is with! I can't see them going together!" about a pair who have just entered.

They order more beers and they watch and gossip, and they roll the wax from the dripping candles into balls, and the music plays on:

> . . . *why can't I have love like that brought to me,*
> *something to live for, something to live for . . .*

Now and then, like tonight, a group like those at Jackie and Connie's table become titillated by another group who enters—a group from uptown. Olivia's group.

With great subtlety, they alert one another.

"Look what just came in."

"Get them!"

Or: "Don't look now, but—"

Dressed in heels and hose, Olivia and Tanja, Jane Allen and Deenie stroll to a table.

The two groups are acquainted, but there is little love between them. If they speak at all, it is an apathetic "Hi" they exchange. The uptown group pretends to be slumming; the downtown group pretends there is a sudden bad odor in The Dock.

Sometimes there exists a mild friendship between the two girls, each from the other group. This is true between Janie

Allen and Cynthia Fullerton. A few years ago, they were lovers, when Janie lived down on Waverly Place.

Janie stops at the table where Cynthia sits, en route to the ladies' room.

Cynthia says, "How are things uptown?"

"Just fine!" Jane replies. "We got a Hillman Mynx."

"They're great little cars," says Cynthia. The others are mute, drinking their beer with feigned disinterest. "What year is it?"

"Oh, it's new."

"Oh."

"We love it!"

Cynthia says again, "They're great little cars."

"Nice to see you," Jane says. "Still in photography?"

"Yes. I'm doing well."

"Good . . . Well, nice seeing you. Take care."

Cynthia says, "You too."

When Jane Allen is out of sight, Jackie says: "Oh, it's new!" imitating Jane's tone.

Cynthia's girl friend Selma says: "She said *still in photography* as though you were an odd-jobs bum. You've always been in photography!"

"She's all right," Cynthia answers. "Really!"

Selma says, "Do you wish you were still going with her?"

"Oh, come on, Selma. Don't be that way!"

"How old is she anyway?" Selma says. "She looks forty."

Cynthia snaps, "She looks darn good and you know it!"

"Well, why don't you go back with her then?"

"You make me sick, Selma!"

"And you make me sicker!"

Thus, the pair who vowed never to fight the way they do join Jackie, Connie, Doris and Lou in a general atmosphere of grumpiness. More beer is ordered. The song plays on:

. . . something to live for . . . something to live for . . .

And back at Olivia's table? The situation is different, but not much better. There, the foursome is restless and bored. Olivia insists the bar is not sending back Vat 69, as she requested; the Scotch they served her is vile! Deenie doesn't like bars like these—they depress her. Jane Allen says, "Good Lord, don't you have any sense of humor?" Tanja, on the other hand, is fascinated. She can't take her eyes off Kit, at the end of the bar.

Olivia says, "For God's sake, where's your taste? No wonder your analyst thinks you're a goddam masochist!"

"Let's go somewhere we can dance!" Jane says. "Let's go around the corner to the Three Flights Up!"

Deenie whines, "I hate that place! All the transvestites are there!"

"So *what*!"

"Yes, let's *do* get out of here!" Olivia agrees. "At least the place around the corner is amusing."

Tanja is staring at Kit, and now Kit notices her.

"Come on!" Olivia says, "The Scotch is vile in here!"

"Come *on*!" Janie Allen says.

The gay girls gather up their wallets, drop their tips on the tables and push on—to be seen more on the never-ending, frustrating search for something different.

"Let's go around the corner to the Three Flights Up!" Cynthia Fullerton says.

Selma says, "I thought we were going to have only one drink, and then go home."

"I don't feel like it now. Come on, let's go someplace else."

And Kit, at the end of the bar, asks one of the four girls sitting there, "Did you see that kid who just left? Who is she, do you know?"

"Can't help you, honey," is the answer.

Kit looks wistfully at the door through which Tanja passed with Olivia.

At the entrance to Three Flights Up, there is a tall, husky man guarding the door. This bar caters exclusively to the Lesbian. Men accompanied by Lesbians are the only men allowed.

This bar is owned and operated by a Lesbian named Agnes. She is a short, wiry woman in her late forties with a sharp tongue and a low tolerance of any funny business.

Funny business includes males who want to crash the bar; girls who try to nurse one beer for three hours; parties who walk out on a check; girls who monopolize the pay phone; and waitresses who sit down with customers at tables.

Three Flights Up is on the third floor of a rickety building east of Sixth Avenue in Greenwich Village. It is a small, dirty, brightly lit bar with a blaring jukebox, an area for dancing, and tables lining the wall.

The dancing is the attraction; and the floor is always crowded.

The Cha-Cha, The Fish, and the inevitable slow torch song are the favorites.

Frenchy, a waitress in this bar, told me an interesting story when I had coffee with her one night after work. Frenchy looks like a young boy. A semitransvestite, she has always worn men's pants and a shirt, though she doesn't own a suit and doesn't wear men's underwear. She wears her hair in the short bob typical of many girls like her. It is not a man's haircut, simply a bob. She looks like a clean-cut, red-cheeked Jimmy Dean or Tommy Sands. She appears shy and slightly self-conscious. Actually, she is not very innocent. Her girl friend is a striptease artist who works a joint on 3rd Street. Before that, Frenchy hung around with a bunch who worked at a gay club in Miami.

Frenchy is twenty-four. Her mother was a Lesbian. She

has never been with a man, never been remotely interested in a man. Men make her nervous and embarrassed.

Frenchy's story is concerned with the night Agnes announced to all the waitresses in Three Flights Up that they would have to wear skirts. There was some sort of outside pressure responsible for the change in policy.

"I wanted to die," Frenchy said. "I felt as though I would look as unnatural in a skirt as a man would. I remember that night I went to work in pants, and carried the skirt in a bag. I changed in the bathroom. All the while I worked I felt self-conscious and silly."

There was a man in The Three Flights Up—a brother of one of the girls. He was a pleasant fellow, who had long ago accepted the fact that his sister was a Lesbian. Periodically when he came to town, he visited the gay bars with her.

Frenchy was waiting on their table. The fellow was friendly, and because it was a Monday night, and not very busy, Frenchy talked a little with him.

"Then out of a clear blue sky," Frenchy told me, "he complimented me on my legs. He said I had very beautiful legs, like Marlene Dietrich's. I thought he was teasing me, and I was a little peeved, but he was sincere. He said all I had to do was to look in a mirror."

Frenchy had never thought about her legs before one way or the other. When she returned home, her girl friend was asleep. Frenchy stood before the mirror and thought of herself as a woman.

"It was so funny," she said, "I never thought of myself that way. My girl was the lady. She is beautiful—everyone says so. But me? I was always the boy. I stood there thinking about the way I would look in a dress, with heels, with my hair longer. My legs are nice. The fellow was right. I stood at the mirror wondering what it would have been like if I had grown up like a normal girl. I had never thought that before. Then, my girl

woke up. She called me into the bedroom, beckoned me over
to her. She said 'For the love of Jesus, honey, get the skirt off! I
can't bear you in women's clothing!' I took the skirt off and
went to bed. After we made love, I had a cigarette. I lay there
smoking and looking at my skirt in a heap on the floor. I
thought, what a crazy world it is anyway!"

Tonight in Three Flights Up, Frenchy is back in pants. All
the waitresses are. The pressure is off; Agnes arranged the usual
token payment for protection.

Three Flights Up caters to all gay types. There is the curly-
haired, aging dyke on a barstool, a little tight, wearing black
pants and a turtleneck sweater, banging her fist down suddenly on the mahogany bar, declaring to the frowsy blond beside
her: "What the hell do you know? I'm still the best damn P.T.
teacher in the whole East!"

There is the slender, young Puerto Rican girl in the tight
black dress, and the open-toed spikes with the plastic heels,
dancing cheek-to-cheek with the chubby, midget-faced,
woman with a man's haircut, and men's slacks, shoes, and
shirt.

There are two Negro girls, both in dresses and loafers,
doing a fast Cha-Cha, expressionless, provocative.

There is a girl in the corner standing alone, bobbed hair,
pants, a man's V-neck sweater and shirt, a cap tipped across her
forehead, sullen-faced—watching a young redhead who sits at
a table across the room.

She wants to know: "Who's the new face?"

There are Morgan and Miki, the pair from Atlantic City,
with another transvestite and her girl. Morgan and the other
transvestite always use the men's room in the Three Flights Up.

There are these, and then there are Jackie and Connie,
Cynthia and Selma, Doris and Lou. They sit in the rear, by the
window. Across from them at another table are Olivia and
Tanja, Janie Allen and Deenie.

The music is a little louder than it was in The Dock, a little jazzier:

Ew baby, oh, ew, oh, ah, baby—
Ew, say, say, say, oh, say you're mine . . .

The rooms is more jammed than The Dock was. It is brighter, smokier, more frantic. The waitresses hustle more. Beer bottles are picked up before they are even emptied. From behind the bar, Agnes keeps an eagle eye out for funny business. Everyone dances. Miki and Morgan. Selma and Cynthia. Janie and Deenie. It is that point in the evening which few will remember too clearly.

Olivia has gone back to wait her turn in line for the ladies' room.

At a table, Jackie tells Connie: "Happy anniversary!"

"I love you," Connie says. "I just love you."

"I'm sorry about asking that girl over from across the hall."

Connie touches Jackie's cheek. "I just love you," she repeats.

On the dancefloor, Jane Allen says: "I don't think Cynthia's really serious about that girl she's with. Cynthia could be a real nice person if she'd move out of the Village."

Deenie asks, "Do you wish you were still going with her?"

And a few couples behind them, Selma says to Cynthia, "Sometimes I think you wish you were still going with Jane Allen."

It is near closing time. There is a last call shouted by Agnes.

Through the door, bleary-eyed, a little shaky on her feet, comes Kit. She pauses, looking around the room. Then she hears: "Over here."

Kit turns. Tanja, alone at the table, smiles timidly.

"I was looking for you," Kit says.

"I didn't want to leave The Dock," Tanja answers.

They stare at one another for a moment.

Then Tanja says: "Don't stay here. When the woman with me comes back from the ladies' room, I'll meet you there."

"Look," Kit says, steadying herself slightly by holding on to the table. "I think I'm in love with you. I don't even know your name."

"Go back and wait for me," Tanja implores her. "I'll come as soon as I can."

With a dazed expression, clutching a copy of Edna St. Vincent Millay's poems, Kit makes her way back toward the ladies' room.

Janie Allen has seen it all from the dancefloor. "What's that all about?" she says to Deenie.

"Just some drunken character."

"No, it doesn't look that way. Look at the expression in Tanja's eyes. We better tell Olivia."

"Why?"

"Because Olivia is my friend, damn it. She's supporting that kid!"

Again Agnes shouts, "Last Call! Last Call!"

Morgan excuses herself like a proper gentleman as she passes Olivia in the little hallway between the ladies' and men's rooms. Olivia glances at her coldly.

"Don't put on airs with me, bitch," Morgan gives her a lopsided grin. "You're in Three Flights Up just like me, and you're just as queer!"

By the door of the ladies' room Kit waits, leaning against the wall, her eyes shut.

Then she hears Tanja's voice: "I don't have time to talk long now."

"Can you meet me tomorrow?"

"Maybe. But not here. My phone number is on this slip of paper. Call between eleven and four. My friend isn't home then."

Kit takes the paper from her hand, pressing her hand.

"Do you feel something too?" she asks.

Tanja says, "I feel as though I don't care what happens, if I can be with you."

They stand there looking into each other's eyes.

Behind them, Olivia shouts suddenly: "Tanja, we're leaving!"

"I'm coming," Tanja says.

Olivia grabs her and pulls her along. "You're damn right you are, you goddam little neurotic masochist!"

The lights go on suddenly. The music groans to a stop.

"Good night, all!" Agnes shouts. "Closing time!"

There is a mild protest:

"We didn't even finish our beer!"

"It's only ten to four!"

"I didn't hear my song play!"

But Agnes doesn't tolerate funny business.

The waitresses begin to sweep up. The bouncer, in the doorway calls, "Hurry it up! Come on, girls, it's all over but the shouting!"

A line of cabs waits outside.

Morgan holds the door of one for Miki.

Jackie, Connie, Selma, and Cynthia share one, all piling in together.

Lou and Doris are fighting. They tell the others to go on without them.

Lou says, "Am I supposed to put my mother out in the snow when she arrives?"

A Hillman Mynx warms up behind the cabs. "Give us a call, Olly," Janie Allen shouts from the driver's seat. "And Tanja, we really liked your work, no kidding!"

Tanja smiles thinly.

"Come on," Olivia says to her. "Come on, baby. Good God, I didn't mean to yell at you, but it embarrassed me to see you talking with that creep."

She opens the door of her Thunderbird, and Tanja gets in.

The best damn P.T. teacher in the East falls to her knees as she comes down the steps of the bar. The bouncer rushes down to help her up.

The slender Puerto Rican girl in the black dress and the spike heels walks hand and hand down the street with the woman with the man's haircut.

"Good night! Good night!" is the cry at four in the morning as the gay girls break it up.

In the shadows of a doorway, Kit watches until she can no longer see the Thunderbird and the girl in the front seat beside the driver. In the street there is just the dust it made as it cut away, and sped back uptown.

But the precious slip of paper with the telephone number written on it is pressed between the pages of love sonnets.

Kit wanders home in the new day's blue humming:

"Something to live for; something to make my life an adventurous dream . . ."

7.   SISTERS IN THE SUN

1. At Fire Island . . .

Fire Island is a strip of sun-baked land forty miles long, off Long Island. It is accessible only by ferry, and it is divided into about nine separate communities. There are no cars on Fire Island, thus, no roads or paths connecting these communities. One of these, a beautiful spot near the tip of the Island, is a homosexual settlement.

Dr. Robert Caprio, writing in *Female Homosexuality*, states, ". . . it is practically public knowledge that many Lesbians find the island an ideal retreat for their secret love affairs." He tells of one Lesbian whom he interviewed who declared that she could not return to Fire Island, even for a day, because she was afraid it would revive too many painful memories.

Janie Allen, the advertising copywriter, put it another way:

"Fire Island," she said, "is like the Village, in its homosexual part. Only the card-carrying homosexuals frequent it any more. Sure, there was a time when I went there in the summer. But I got sick of it. I got sick of the faggots out there. They outnumber the girls twenty to one, and they're really shameless. It's one big orgy after the other where they're concerned. They hunt each other up and down the boardwalks after dark, and they drink, and fight like girls, and turn the whole place into something like the steam baths. The girls that go there are just as tiresome. They sit around in little knots watching the boys, or dancing together as though they were glued to one another, or back in their cottages they drink and fight. It's just too much. I wouldn't go there again. I like to live in a normal community."

Jackie Spencer, the airlines reservation clerk and would-be playwright, differs with Janie.

"There's no place like it," she says. "Connie and I want to buy a place there eventually. It's the most beautiful spot I know of. Homosexuals who claim they hate it because it's too homosexual must have guilt complexes or something. What the boys do on the island is their business. Personally, I think they're fun."

In the summer, Jackie and Connie, and Cynthia and Selma, rent a cottage in this community on Fire Island. They spend weekends there, and their two-week vacations.

The cottage they rent is about half a mile from the ferry dock. It is owned by a male homosexual who has named it the Gay Receiver. It is across the boardwalk from a cottage named the Summer Cruise, and next door to one named the Greek Treat. Often the names of the cottages in this community have *double-entendres* for the gay crowd.

The Gay Receiver is a two-bedroom pink cottage with a huge picture window in front, and has a white picket fence enclosing it. It is a short distance from the dunes which lead down to the ocean, and a stone's throw from one of the three bars-and-restaurants catering to the community.

During the day, this community tries to look like any other community on Fire Island. There are young men and girls on the beach, and there are children playing in the sand. There are a few older people, too. On first glance, to the outsider, it seems to be typical of any beach resort.

But take a closer look.

It sometimes sounds like a cliché to describe homosexual males as extremely handsome, rather beautiful, or lithe and sensitive-looking. Male homosexuals themselves are often the first to protest that "we don't look any different from anyone else—most of us." Apart from the crowd, this may be true. But with the crowd, in the countless groups that pepper the beach on this part of Fire Island, their homosexuality is unmistakable. They might be mistaken for a group of unusually attractive undergraduates, but observed more closely, one notices a pair involved in intense conversation, touching each other's cheeks and arms as they talk; a pair sleeping close together on their stomachs, their bodies touching; a pair rubbing sun oil on each other and giggling; and not uncommonly, though such action is frowned upon by the majority, a pair kissing quickly, in an attitude of playfulness.

The girls on the beach are by no means as many in number. Often they spread their blankets alongside the boys, when they have friends among them, and mixed groups are not at all unusual. Yet despite the specious affection between members of the opposite sex in these groups, it becomes quite obvious that the girls are with the girls, the boys with the boys.

Of course, there are always exceptions. In the minority on the beach at Fire Island are about a score of heterosexuals. Some of them own property there, some are visitors. Many are employed there.

The children one observes on the beach usually belong to this minority. The children are the products of a "gay" marriage, or the victims of divorce, when one member of the marriage was homosexual.

There is something about the atmosphere on this section of Fire Island which makes the Lesbian even more masculine; the male homosexual even more feminine. Naturally, the great aura of freedom has something to do with creating this atmosphere. And then again, there are no "real" women around to remind the male of his masculine role; and no "real" men to remind the woman of her feminine role.

Let's go along the beach with Jackie Spenser and Connie, who are joining two gay boys in a hollow just below the dunes.

Les and Vincent are waiting for the couple, blankets spread out, portable radio tuned to pop music, and beer in the plastic, insulated container.

Les wears a one-piece striped suit, the old-fashioned kind which covers him above the waist—high fashion this summer. Vincent wears a very abbreviated pair of white trunks. Jackie and Connie both wear two-piece suits.

The four sit sipping beer and listening to music, talking about the terrible aircrash they heard of over the news, and about each other's jobs. Les is a window decorator for one of the large department stores in New York City. Vincent is a salesman with an ad agency in the city. Les is the more passive of the pair. Every now and then Vincent reminds him that he sunburns easily.

Jackie says, "So does Connie, but try to tell them anything!"

It is as though the two men were discussing their wives, or their girls.

At one point, Connie decides to go swimming.

"I wouldn't do it, honey," Jackie says. "We've just eaten lunch."

"It's been over half an hour!"

"Will you please listen to me? I want you to wait, honey."

Vincent says, "Why don't you wait, doll? It won't hurt."

Les says: "Oh, they're such worry warts, huh, Con?"

"C'mon, Les come with me," Connie says.

Vincent touches Connie's arm. "Really," he tells her, "Les ought to go back to the cottage and get a shirt. He burns very easily."

Les says, "I feel like swimming!"

Defiantly, hand in hand, Les and Connie run laughing toward the water.

Vincent tells Jackie: "I'm really worried about his shoulders and arms. He burns very easily!"

"It hasn't been half an hour since we ate," Jackie answers. "I could kill her. She shouldn't go in!"

They watch the pair momentarily, lighting cigarettes.

Vincent asks, "Is everything going all right between you two?"

"It's been over a year now."

"I'm so pleased!"

"How about you?" Jackie asks.

Vincent sighs. "He's just a kid, Jackie, you know? He doesn't mean to hurt me, but he can't help it. He's only twenty. And out here everyone's after him. I don't know why I brought him out here. Next year we're going to East Hampton."

"If I were a man, I'd never bring another man out here."

"It's terrible! Look at him, he's just a kid! I know he's going to have an awful burn, but when I tell him, he tells me I nag him."

Jackie says, "I ought to go down there and yank her out of the water by her hair! She should know better! It's been only fifteen minutes since we had lunch!"

After their romp in the surf, Connie and Les take a walk down the beach.

Les says, "He'll be furious with me!"

"They're like two mother hens," Connie laughs.

"He's a very jealous person, Con. Is Jackie?"

"Sort of. She doesn't have any reason."

"You really like her, hmmm?"

"We've been together over a year now."

Les says, "I don't know whether I could stay that long with anyone or not. The trouble with me is that I don't *want* to settle down. I'm young, and I like fun."

"Boys are different anyway, I guess."

"I even like girls," Les says. "I mean, I'm not ready yet to say I'm completely queer. Do you know what I mean?"

"I know. I used to feel that way when I was younger."

"Vincent is thirty-six. I'm young. How do I know that I might not want kids? I like kids."

"I do too."

"I was with a woman once. I didn't mind it. Sometimes I like the idea of being with a woman. Vincent says I pretend that, but I mean it, Con."

"I think you should have a chance to find out, Les."

"I know it. It isn't fair."

"I've tried with men, but I just don't like them as well as women—in bed."

"I adore men," Lester tells her, "but I like to be around women. Vincent is different. He isn't too fond of women. Oh, he likes you and Jackie, but you know what I mean."

"I know," Connie says thoughtfully. "Jackie's that way too. I wish sometimes we'd go out with some gay boys, but Jackie says they bore her."

"We ought to get together on our own, when we get back to New York."

"Sure," Connie answers. "Why not? Want to?"

"We could have cocktails or even dinner now and then."

"I'd love it," Connie squeezes his arm.

"We'll do it, Con. The hell with them!"

An hour later, when they return to the blanket to rejoin Vincent and Jackie, Vincent stands up.

He says to Les, "We're going straight to the cottage, and I'm going to rub some cream on you. Les, you're just bright red! You know you burn easily!"

Les shrugs.

"C'mon now, Les. Please, darling. I'm worried sick!"

Les agrees.

They say good-by to the girls, and start back up the dunes.

For a while the girls are silent.

Then Jackie snarls: "What were you trying to prove?"

"You mean because I didn't obey you?"

"You're a goddam faggot-chaser," Jackie says. "You make me sick!"

"And you're a little Hitler!" Connie answers.

The afternoon sun beats down on the pair, the radio plays show tunes, and the day nears evening.

Night on Fire Island—in this community: the bars, by eight-thirty, are beginning to fill. Dotting the walks are the cottages, lit by candles and kerosene lamps. The jukeboxes roar; the pianos bang; the surf pounds, and the moon is rising, a round globe in the east.

There are men everywhere, young and old. On the beach, a jeep which acts as a taxi, lets off visitors from other spots on the island, who have come to see the "queers." In the restaurants, cocktails and dinners are downed, candles flicker. By ten-thirty the bars are jammed. Those who have had dinner in their cottages begin to trek to the bars along the boardwalks.

On the bay side there is a huge hotel; downstairs, inside— a long bar and a room for dancing. There are pool tables, miniature bowling machines, and pinball machines.

There are men everywhere.

At the bar, a pair of tourists from Ocean Beach, on Fire Island, talk to two of the boys.

"You're so young for all of this," the woman says to one.

The boy giggles and puts his arm around his companion's waist. He says to the woman: "Well, weren't you a young bride yourself?"

The woman shakes her head. "You both ought to be spanked!"

The boys giggle hilariously, and the woman's husband says to her: "Stop making an idiot out of yourself. Let's go back to Ocean Beach!"

Usually the boys are not allowed to dance together, but tonight they do. It is early in the season; the rules are more elastic.

The floor is jammed with them.

There are a few Lesbians dancing together, too. At a table in the corner, there are about eleven Lesbians sitting together, watching. Occasionally, one of the boys dances with one of the girls.

Tonight Jackie Spenser dances with Vincent.

"It was just the way I thought it would be," he tells Jackie. "He got a terrible burn. I just suffer for him. He's bright red!"

"We had a little fight," Jackie says, "but we patched it up. God, women can be problems!"

Vincent says: "And you don't think *men* can be?"

Many couples away, Connie and Les dance.

"I don't know what to *do*," Les says. "He keeps eying me. At the bar he was nudging my elbow like mad! He *knows* I'm with Vincent, but he's so bold! Look at him—isn't he handsome?"

"He's cute," Connie agrees.

"Oh, he's fierce! I don't know what to do!"

On the sidelines, with a crowd of others who are watching the dancing, a young man with a good tan, wearing white shorts and a blue shirt open to show his chest, watches Les and Connie like a hawk.

Behind him, a girl with her arm linked in a boy's says: "I'm so glad we came! I've never seen anything like this in my entire life!"

"It makes me want to puke," the boy answers.

A slender, pretty boy standing beside him says: "Methinks you do protest too much."

Eleven o'clock, twelve o'clock, one o'clock—and the empty beer cases pile up behind the bar. Voices grow louder, and higher; the bars are mobbed now. In some places there is barely room to move. Outside, along the walks and on the beach, boy with boy, man with boy, and now and then, girl with girl, are walking with their arms tightly around each other. From various cottages come the noise of parties—more drinking, more dancing, more love-tender meetings and male-urgent rendezvous.

At two o'clock on the beach, the jeep taxis wait to take the roving tourists back to their own communities on the island.

A boy asks a jeep driver: "Been driving long?"

The jeep driver laughs. "Long *enough*."

"Sure?" the boy smiles seductively.

"You're wasting your time, lad."

The boy disappears back up the dunes.

A piano player in one of the bars plays Noel Coward tunes. Someone requests "We're Rotten To The Core" and everyone claps approval.

The piano player sings as he plays:

Darling we're really rotten to the core,
It's funny that I've never thought of it before—

Back at the hotel, at two o'clock, Vincent approaches Jackie and Connie as they are leaving for their cottage.

"Did you see him?"

"No," Jackie says.

"You were dancing with him, Connie. I haven't seen him since!"

Connie tells him, "We only had three dances. Then he excused himself."

"I just hope he's not sick some place. I mean, he really has a vile sunburn."

"I don't think he's sick some place," Connie says.

"Then he's with someone?"

"I don't know, Vincent."

"That little bitch! That rotten little bitch!"

The girls leave Vincent, and head down the boardwalk toward the Gay Receiver. The moon is a yellow circle in the sky above; the blackness is star-splotched.

"Look," Connie whispers, "there's Les."

They see him heading toward the dunes with the boy who had been watching him.

"I'm glad we're not like the faggots," Jackie says.

From the bushes a high voice squeaks: "We're glad you're not too, dykes!"

2. At the Hamptons . . .

"Last summer our landlady at the Hampton Bays was quite shocked by us," Janie Allen told me. "She thought Deenie and I were living in sin with Greg and Philo."

This is a common way for the Lesbians and male homosexuals to detract attention from themselves in a normal community during the summer. Two Lesbians rent a cottage with two gay boys.

Greg, a publicity man for a charity organization, said: "It's very practical all the way around. I could invite friends from the office out, and feel completely at ease, because the girls were there. In the city, friends from the office very seldom expect an invitation to your home, but in the summer, if you have a cottage, it often is expected of you. Philo and Deenie just carried on as though they were in the throes of passion, and Janie and I acted as though we were engaged."

Deenie added: "My folks came to visit us and they were crazy about Philo. They were so pleased that I seemed seriously interested in a man, at last, that they didn't even remark on the fact we were unchaperoned at the cottage."

Janie and Deenie took the cottage with the boys at Hampton Bays, and at South Hampton Tay and Huguette shared a cottage with two male actors.

"We got together a lot during the summer, the eight of us," Janie said, "and most of the time we were at cocktail parties and bars and restaurants, and on the beach with normal people. It's boring to be just with homosexuals. When you are, there's a tendency to act like little kids left at home to raise hell when the parents are away. It gets too frantic and wild. I like the check of normal people. I like to feel I'm a part of a normal life, not some character people point out."

Sometimes the "normal life" in the Hamptons can bemuse even the homosexual, in its elasticity. An incident that happened to Janie and Deenie, Greg and Philo illustrates this.

"We led a pretty quiet life out there," Janie said, "but now and then we were invited to big parties. The boys Tay and Huguette shared their cottage with knew all the theatrical people in the Hamptons, and one Saturday night we were invited to a party out in Bridgehampton, given by Mimosa, the actress, who was in summer stock there."

The foursome went to Mimosa's party and stayed very late, enjoying themselves thoroughly, drinking Scotch and mingling with the other "names." Gradually the crowd began to thin out, and Mimosa got a little more tight with each drink. She began to fix her attention on Deenie and Janie Allen, asking both to kiss her. Each one complied, and after many more rounds of drinks, when Philo and Greg suggested leaving, Mimosa begged the girls not to go yet. The boys left, getting a ride with another couple, leaving the car behind so the girls could stay longer.

There had been no mention of homosexuality the whole evening; and no indication that anyone there was gay. It was a very straight party, save for the fact that toward the end, Mimosa felt like being kissed by the two girls.

As the trio drank more and more, Mimosa focused her attention completely on Deenie. She asked Deenie to go into the bedroom with her and talk, and left Janie in the living room listening to the record-player. Janie dozed a little, but woke up at one point to hear Mimosa shouting: "Darling, would you be a lamb and bring us some ice cubes!"

When Janie carried the ice cubes into the bedroom, she found Deenie, quite drunk, her blouse open, lying in Mimosa's arms. Both had lipstick all over their faces.

Janie felt very depressed, and a little peeved.

"What's the matter, darling," Mimosa said. "You look sad."

Janie said, "I am."

"But *why* on earth, darling."

"Well, I'm afraid this is going to cause a fight between Deenie and me and no one enjoys a fight."

"Then, don't fight, darling! Good Lord, you're so serious!"

"I like Deenie very much," Janie said solemnly. "In fact, I *love* Deenie."

At this, Mimosa sat up in bed like a shot.

"Oh, good God!" she moaned. "Don't tell me you're Lesbians!"

3. At Riis Park . . .

Those who cannot afford the luxury of a cottage at Fire Island, in the Hamptons, or anywhere else out of town, have Riis Park to visit.

"It's one big camp," Fortune Secora says. "You just get on the subway and head for that beach. The gay boys cruise it like crazy, and don't think the girls don't too. I always see someone from The Dock, or the Three Flights Up out there. There's one part of Riis Park that just screams gay."

When Miki and Morgan do not have jobs in clubs at Atlantic City for the summer, Riis Park is their summer hang-out.

Morgan told me: "Out there I don't feel funny. You go to Jones Beach or Coney Island, and you feel funny if you're different. But at Riis Park there're plenty like me. We all wear two-piece suits with a T-shirt over the top, when we're not in the water. That way we just seem like a lot of guys—in trunks with a T-shirt."

"They're not fooling anyone," Miki added, "because it's awful hard for a dyke to look like a man in a bathing suit. But out at Riis, they feel as though they fit in. There are so many dykes out there, and so many screaming faggots, it's a ball."

Riis Park is just another public beach to the casual observer, but to the gay crowd, less affluent than the Jackie Spencers or the Janie Allen's, it is *their* summer camp.

I have had sexual relations in almost every way it is done. After I had been with several men I was no longer curious about anything male. Still I kept on. One man right after another. Sometimes I would have sexual relations with two men at the same time. How could I have been so immoral? If I had enjoyed intercourse with men, if I had really desired men, I could understand. But I did not. I wanted a woman . . .

This is Mrs. Francis Elliot speaking. Her case is recorded by Dr. Benjamin Karpman in his study *The Alcoholic Woman.*

Mrs. Elliot was an alcoholic who was attempting to combat and smother her true homosexual inclinations with an interminable series of heterosexual experiences.

Karpman, in his discussion of her case, was almost surprised at the "obstinancy" with which this woman fought off her homosexual inclinations, and "the overemphasis which she placed upon the social opprobrium" attached to homosexuality.

It seemed to Karpman bewildering that Mrs. Elliot regarded discovery as a homosexual worse than her plight as a promiscuous, hopeless alcoholic.

Should this be so surprising?

Today, innumerable women have "come through the rye"

carrying manuscripts recording their shocking and degrading experiences as alcoholics. The sensation-hungry public has received them with open arms, paid to read their stories, to see the movies of their lives, to hear them make their comebacks on the café circuits. Today the reformed alcoholic woman has almost as much glamour appeal as the purple heart veteran had back in the late 40's.

One very drunken hag, holding herself up at a bar in the West 50's one night, said to me: "One of these days I'm going to sober up and write about my goddam life. Could get Bette Davis to do the movie. Used to look a lot like her, I did."

Wouldn't most women today rather be called an alcoholic than a Lesbian?

Lesbians cannot join any organization, publicly supported and approved, which puts all its efforts into studying the problem of homosexuality, as Alcoholics Anonymous offers to the problem drinker.

Did Mrs. Francis Elliot overemphasize the social opprobrium attached to homosexuality, as Dr. Karpman thinks? I doubt it.

One Lesbian I know told me this:

"My mother said to me: 'Evelyn, if you were only a drunk or a dope addict or something, I think your father and I could understand. Youngsters often get in trouble. But how are we supposed to understand a Lesbian?'"

Another Lesbian said, "My older sister said she wished there was an organization like A.A. to help me. I teased her. I said, 'Oh, don't you know? There is. It's called H.A. If ever a homosexual gets the urge she just calls up H.A. and they send over someone right away to sit and drink with her all night.'"

The Lesbians joke about the imaginary organization called Homosexuals Anonymous, who will send someone over to drink all night with a Lesbian, to keep her from another woman, has behind it an unconscious kernel of truth where

82

society is concerned. It is better to be a drunk, than to be a queer.

Too often, Lesbians are both. There is very little release offered the homosexual in the way of advice, direction, or sympathetic understanding, from parents, priests, teachers, or even from friends, business colleagues, or neighbors.

Of course, there is always the psychiatrist. In the next chapter analysis and analysands will be discussed. For the present, let's look more closely at the relationship of liquor to Lesbians.

As Dr. Karpman pointed out, Lesbianism drove Mrs. Francis Elliot to drink. Karpman, Caprio, Henry and many other doctors have pointed this out: many women drink to excess in order to tolerate sexual relations with men, thus attempting to prove they are not abnormal.

A girl I went through college with, a wild type who drank and had a reputation for promiscuity with men, met me in The Dock several years after we were both graduated. My first reaction was complete surprise at seeing her there; my second, at seeing that she was drinking orange juice.

"I'm A.A.," she said. "I finally straightened myself out. But God, how I regret those years in school. I was so damned scared. I thought everyone suspected me, even though I was always with men. I made a point never to be too close with girls. I'd had one experience with an older woman when I was in my teens, and I could never forget it. I loved her and hated her, and I was so ashamed. There was no one to go to and tell—just no one!"

The girl came from a small town in Missouri. She could not go to the family doctor, or her minister, or her parents, or her friends.

"In college," she said, "I wanted to go to my psych teacher and talk to him. But I was always afraid he'd tell the other faculty members, or my housemother, or the dean. I didn't think I could trust anyone. So I started having affairs with all the men I could, and I drank for nerve. I was a mess! No one respected me—I knew that, but I thought it was better than being thought of as a Lesbian. I even had an abortion."

Since college, the girl has settled in San Francisco. She met a gay boy there and married him.

"We live in a gay world," she said. "I have my affairs with girls, and he has his with boys. It's not perfect, but it's so much better than what I went through at school! I cut the drinking completely out. My husband and I never pretend any physical attraction; we've never had sex. But we understand each other, and help each other."

If many Lesbians turn to liquor to tolerate sexual relations with men, probably a good many, too, drink to tolerate sexual relations with women.

Kathleen, a homosexual case reported on in *All The Sexes* by Dr. George W. Henry, was unable to yield to the advances of an aggressive Lesbian until she got drunk. After living with another woman for four years in a homosexual relationship, she showed her disillusionment by excessive drinking.

Huguette, the French girl who lives with her boss, Miss Taylor, told me: "Usually I have a drink or two before making love, often more, enough to make me a little heady. I feel strange without the stimulus, and sometimes I feel impossible to be like that with another woman. I have made love without liquor, but I didn't enjoy it so much. I am not a big drinker at all—but just at those times it helps."

Dr. Robert Caprio in *Female Homosexuality*, discussing the role of alcohol in homosexuality, tells of an attorney's wife, who, whenever the attorney had occasion to be away for a weekend, asked a close woman friend to spend the night with her. Each time they met, they would drink great amounts, and then commence "sexual indulgences which consisted of tribadism and occasional cunnilingus."

Morgan, the transvestite who goes with Miki, claims: "A shot or two a night doesn't make me a drunk, but it does make me a good lover. It relaxes me."

"It makes her feel more masculine," Miki said; "makes her believe in herself more. One of Morgan's biggest problems is believing she's what she tries to be—a man."

One Lesbian with whom I discussed alcohol told me: "The girl I go with loves to go to the bars and drink whenever she can, whenever we have the money. She looks at all the girls, and she acts very affectionate toward me, and she seems completely happy. But she always gets terribly drunk—too drunk to make love when we get back home, and too hungover to do it the next day. I think she drinks to avoid sex."

Some homosexuals, then, drink to run away from homosexuality; some drink to enjoy it; and some drink to avoid the actual sex act—thus live as homosexuals without suffering the feeling of guilt or inadequacy in the physical side of the relationship.

While actual alcoholism is a problem only for the few among Lesbians, liquor is quite commonly a problem for the many.

Dr. George W. Henry, writing in *All The Sexes*, says: "Bacchus makes his strongest appeal to feminine men and masculine women."

A doctor with whom I was discussing this said: "The woman who drinks too much is almost always coping with sexual inadequacy. In a sense, she is saying 'I don't want to be grown up. I want to be a child again, protected from the responsibility of the female.' Liquor offers her a false sense of security—a sense of benevolent protection from fear, guilt, etc." He added, "Look at a drunken woman and see how like a child she has become. She cannot walk steady. She spills drinks and soils herself. She cannot talk clearly, or think with much logic. Sometimes she cries, rages, quarrels, or sinks into a state of dreamy stupor. In a word, she has made herself helpless."

I thought of a wild-looking, fiftyish, masculine woman in a woman's tailored pinstripe suit, standing by the jukebox in The Dock one night, suddenly breaking into a fantastically crazy dance, snapping her fingers and clapping her hands—jumping up and down like a goofy five-year-old showing off before company, singing: "*Yessir, she's my baby—ah, no sir, don't mean maybe—*" I thought of half a dozen grown women gathered around a table, playing poker and drinking Scotch, suddenly drunker, acting more and more like the tomboys of twenty years past, their poker game interspersed with such comments as: "Screw you!" "Bet your ass, baby!" "Up yours with a meat hook!" "Aw, shit!"—all of them, women with responsible, high-paying jobs in such media as advertising, book publishing, television or magazine fashions.

I thought of fights between Lesbians under the influence of alcohol, wild, rough affairs with blows exchanged; of the stunned and glazed expressions of the gamine-types in bermuda shorts, stumbling their way down some Village street after an evening with friends, looking for all the world like lost little boys who had just had their first cigar behind the barn and were still ill from it. I thought of a beautiful singer I know who wept because "I think my girl's leaving me," taking out her contact lenses so she could cry, then losing them as they fell from her lap. I remember her crawling about on all fours under a table at the nightclub where she sang, sobbing: "I'm older than I look. I can't even see without these things. I'm over forty and I gave that kid my best years. Now she just walks out. You don't get relocated that easily after forty!"

The Lesbian, drinking, is never at her best. Yet even knowing this, she will in many instances look to the bottom of the bottle for some release from the awful monotony of being gay. There, she may see that special someone—the woman who is going to be different from all the others, exciting, beautiful, loyal, capable and lasting, the one she will spend the rest of her life with—see her through a blur of alcohol across a crowded room for a sudden moment of inebriated bliss. Or she may see, in the bottom of the bottle, the potentials of her talent suddenly become real, remaking her life—giving her the fame and fortune to take her out of the private hell into which the contents of the bottle invariably thrust her. In the bottom of the bottle she may see the past—the nebulous time when she was not so deeply involved in gay life, before she joined the ranks, when she was young and not so thoroughly initiated into the peculiar mores of her clan.

Some day, if she has seen the bottom of the bottle too often, with too many painful results, she may join A.A. More often, the real problem drinker who is a Lesbian will continue her battle with the bottle.

As one ex-A.A. member told me: "I began to drink because I was a Lesbian and I felt depressed at the way my life was going. I couldn't seem to live with a girl, and I couldn't seem to live without one. So I drank. Then I began to feel depressed at the way I drank. I joined A.A. and didn't drink any more for a while. Well, my life wasn't going any better. I was still a Lesbian, and I still couldn't seem to live with a girl or without one. I got so keyed up I had to go back to drinking."

Another "sometimes A.A." member said this:

"I joined A.A. and met a wonderful woman. I fell deeply in love with her. I didn't drink at all. I wanted to be sober because of her. One night when we were together I couldn't help myself. I made a pass at her. She was pretty mean about it. She said I just gave up liquor because I was a queer and I knew she wouldn't have anything to do with me if I drank. Sure, that's probably true. I had to do it for someone—for some reason. Otherwise, it didn't make sense."

Society has become increasingly generous in its empathetic approach to the problems of the alcoholic and the heavy drinker. Perhaps one day it will extend its empathy to the problems of the homosexual. In a sense, treating alcoholism as it is treated in organizations such as A.A. is equivalent to teaching an undiagnosed blind case how to read Braille, never wondering about the reasons for blindness, or the potentialities for seeing again.

9.   THE FIFTY-MINUTE POWER

Dr. Edmund Bergler, writing in his recent study *Homosexuality: Disease Or Way of Life?*, states emphatically that "there is nothing glamorous about suffering from the disease of homosexuality."

There is nothing glamorous about suffering from *any* disease.

There is nothing glamorous about suffering from any symptom, either, and a majority of psychiatrists today will agree that Lesbianism, as Dr. Frank Caprio put it, "is a symptom, and not a disease entity."

To quote Caprio:

> It is the result of a deep-seated neurosis which involves narcissistic gratifications and sexual immaturity. It also represents a neurotic defense mechanism for feelings of insecurity—a compromise solution for unresolved conflicts involving the relationship during childhood and adolescence to one's parents.

There are many Lesbians who become irate at the idea they are judged as neurotics, or sexually immature people.

"So I prefer to make love to someone of my own sex!" one told me. "Is that anyone's business but mine? Does that make me neurotic?"

The answer to her questions are obvious: it is no one's business unless she makes it someone else's business. It cannot be called a neurosis unless it manifests itself as one. Obviously the Lesbian who is able to quietly settle down with a member of her own sex, and in no way distinguish herself from members of normal society (save by her sexual life, which is conducted in privacy) can certainly find acceptance as a completely normal person. Who's to know, or to care?

The reason homosexuality is regarded as a neurosis is that it is almost impossible for the Lesbian to do this. In the small town, it is difficult to come by a partner, and the choice of the right kind of person is limited. In a small town, it is hard to go against the grain, when everything conventional around the homosexual breeds guilt in her mind, makes her feel out of place with her child-bearing contemporaries, or if she is married and carrying on a risky affair on the side. If she is a homosexual in a small town who is aware of her abnormality, and unable to find overt expression, or concrete help and direction, she is very likely a totally miserable person. Too often the Lesbian in the metropolitan areas calls attention to herself by making it other people's business by visiting gay bars, dressing in a "Greenwich Village uniform," being indiscreet in public places, "confessing" to friends, and relatives, or gathering exclusively with her own kind, causing suspicion among normal persons.

There is no reason I can think of why a Lesbian shouldn't do any, or all of the above, if such is her inclination. Neither is there any reason why the Lesbian should aspire to acceptance as a normal person. She just isn't.

It doesn't necessarily follow that she is a freak, though sometimes she does her best to give this impression. Neither does it follow that because she is a Lesbian, she is necessarily suffering from a disease and leading an unglamorous life. Many Lesbians I know live very glamorous lives, which have nothing at all to do with the fact they are homosexuals.

But what of the Lesbian who *is* suffering? What makes her suffer?

It is usually not so much the need to have society accept her as one with the heterosexual. It is usually the need for the Lesbian to accept herself.

One Lesbian told me: "I am not happy with gay people, because I do not like myself when I am with them. When I am with straight people I am able to like myself much better."

Tanja, the aspirant artist who is kept by Olivia, said about her analysis: "I used to feel guilty about making love with Olivia. She was my first lover, male or female. Even though I traveled with people who were all gay, and all nice people, inside myself I didn't feel right. Olivia sent me to an analyst to get adjusted to the life. I really want to be gay without guilt, but I don't know if that's possible."

Laurie, a very attractive divorcée who has always been a homosexual, and who married to allay suspicion, now has an affair with an equally feminine woman named Clara.

"It's all right when we stay home," Laurie said, "but when we go out to have dinner, or when we get tickets to the theater or the symphony, I always feel self-conscious about being with Clara. I know I imagine it, but I always think people are watching us. Then I get these unbearable migraine headaches and have to go home."

In a small town, the Lesbian who is *suffering* has a tough time of it. Psychiatric help is very limited, and even when it is available, there is considerable reluctance to consult a doctor who may be your neighbor. Homosexuality is an electric word in the small town; an anathema.

In a later chapter I shall quote from letters received by homosexuals from small towns, who wrote in response to my book *We Walk Alone*.

When psychiatrists, analysts, sociologists and the like write optimistically about the effective means of treating sexual inversion, they rarely deal with constructive suggestions for making these means available to those who live far away from metropolitan areas.

Today, there is simply no way of helping the Lesbian in Newark, Ohio; Geneva, New York; Paris, Missouri; Montpelier, Vermont; or like places.

In New York City, and other large areas, the situation is quite the contrary.

Behind the façade of the uptown sports-car driving, poodle-walking cliques, the Greenwich Village Bohemian "bit," the transvestite-femme circle—despite the address, or the costume, or the customs, there are always a good many Lesbians who could benefit by psychiatric help, who, in fact, express their interest in being helped in a variety of ways.

Some say: "I can't afford it, or I would."

Some say: "I don't know how to go about it."

Some say: "How can I be sure I'd go to the right doctor?"

And some, by their vehement reaction against the very idea of psychoanalysis, protest too much.

For the Lesbian who is ill-adjusted in society, and who lives in a metropolitan area, there is help when she admits she needs it. She may be slow to admit that homosexuality is her problem. How many times I've heard gay girls say: "But that's the least of my worries!" Sometimes these girls drink too much, sometimes they suffer from migraine headaches, insomnia, digestive disturbances, depression fits and like complaints. Sometimes they have trouble in their jobs, sometimes in their gay relationships. Still, they insist that homosexuality is not the cause of their difficulties. They look upon analysis as an admission of defeat in the gay arena where they have become warriors for their right to live unencumbered by popular conceptions of the homosexual's tragedies.

Many times, instead of searching their hearts to find out what they are actually getting out of life, instead of asking themselves if their lives can have *more* meaning, they defend life as a homosexual by insisting:

"Heterosexuals are all squares! They aren't as much on the qui vive as gay people are!" "There are so many people in the arts and theater who are gay! Heterosexuals just aren't as creative!" "Gay people have a better sense of humor than straight people!" "Gay people stay more attractive than straight people; dress better, have more flair!" "Gay people keep up with things more!"

At the same time they desire understanding and sympathy from these uncultured, humorless, unattractive, uninformed, not-with-it squares.

Certainly the Lesbians who conduct themselves in such a way are in the minority; certainly there are a vast majority of Lesbians who have intelligently worked at their problems and sought psychiatric help, and sometimes there are Lesbians who have neither been inclined to sneer at heterosexuals, nor been in dire need of psychiatric consultation. But among many Manhattan female homosexuals there are those whose lives could be enriched by their own admission that they need help.

"Sometimes," a Lesbian remarked to me once, "I am reading in a psychiatric book about help being available for me, and I think: Why not get help? And I decide then and there that I will. But where? Nobody ever says *where*. It's frustrating, and eventually I forget all about getting help."

Here are just a few places the Lesbian living in New York City can visit, or write, or call for information about such help. In most cases, the cost for help is adjusted to the individual's means. Anyone earning a weekly salary can afford analysis.

The William Alanson White Institute
12 East 86 Street

The Karen Horney Clinic
115 East 31 Street

The Theodore Reik Clinic
66 5th Avenue

The Group Psychotherapy Center
108 East 86 Street

The process of becoming an analysand may take time. There are applications to fill out, interview sessions, and the inevitable waiting lists. But once the wheels of progress are set in motion, the person in need of help is on her way to getting it; and once she has received it, she will find the time and the effort spent well worth her trouble.

10.   THE MEN IN THEIR LIVES

1. Joe Forrini . . .

You've seen Joe before. You have seen him eating dinner in the Automat around six in the evening, sitting up by a window where he can watch the street, or sitting at the table facing the door where he can search the faces of the people coming and going, and listen to the bits of conversation at the tables around him. Joe knows the regulars in there just as well as the man at the tobacco counter on the corner knows that Joe smokes Camels, and after dinner buys a pack, and pays a penny for a mint, chocolate-coated and wrapped in tin foil.

You've seen Joe on a bench in the park, reading his newspaper or working the crossword puzzle, or simply watching again—always watching other people.

You've seen him in line at the local movie house; seen him in the neighborhood bar nursing a beer and watching television; seen him at the neighborhood store buying fruit to munch on in his room; and seen him from your vantage spot on the street—an anonymous-looking figure up above you in his rented room, wandering about in the glare of the naked electric light bulb that hangs by a cord from the ceiling.

You've never known his name or anything about him, but you have seen the Joes of Manhattan and wondered at their lives, guessed at their loneliness, and pondered the reasons for life's leaving them out—these men who are almost old and very much alone.

Joe Forrini doesn't know the reasons himself. He cannot account for himself or for what his life has become, any more than he can account for the fact that somewhere in his late twenties he began to take on weight in unusual amounts, he began to lose hair; he began to become more and more absorbed in the newspapers, reading sometimes four or five a day; he began to avoid paying visits to his old neighborhood down on Mulberry Street—where his parents had lived until their death; and he began to stop writing his brother Louie, out in California.

Joe Forrini is fifty-eight now. He's as fat as ever, and totally bald. He works as a printer's assistant, and lives a few blocks from where he works, on Bleeker Street in Greenwich Village. In his furnished room there are few personal possessions save for the obvious—clothing, shaving equipment, and a milk bottle in which he saves pennies. Last Christmas his only card was from a liquor store down the street which he patronizes off and on, for jugs of cheap wine to sip on those nights sleep comes slowly.

Until February, Joe led the kind of routine meaningless existence that neither depresses nor elates someone as resigned as Joe. In life, Joe was just *there*—plodding along, noting now and then that yesterday's temperature set a record high, and that they were certainly tearing down a lot of old buildings in the Washington Square area. His disappointments were minor ones—the Automat ran out of baked bean casseroles before he got there, it rained the day after he got a shoe shine, the laundry starched his shirts by mistake. His triumphs were hollow ones: he killed the fly that buzzed about in his room on a hot summer night. The man at Whelan's always remembered his brand of cigarettes. His landlady replaced his old, worn leather spring-popping armchair with a new one.

Joe Forrini was one of the left-over, left-out people of the big city, whose world was a rented room, whose philosophy was a bewildered shrug.

Then one day in February, after he had eaten his dinner, sat in the park, and watched a round of wrestling on television, Joe returned to his room to find a beautiful girl with long pitch-black hair, and sensuous wide red lips, blocking his passage on the stairs.

Joe was afraid of women. He had been with a woman only once, as a kid, forced into it by the other kids. He had been ineffectual and the woman had refused to take his money, even though he begged her to. It would have been less of a disgrace.

That was nearly forty-three years ago. Since then, his dreams were his only sex life, and he could never really remember his dreams. He never daydreamed about women with relation to himself. His day dreams were peopled with strangers, and he was not involved.

His first reaction at seeing the woman was annoyance. He had just bought the early edition of the *News*, and he was looking forward to reading it quietly before he went to sleep. Obviously he had to ask the woman if he could help her. This was an embarrassment as well, for Joe Forrini always imagined that women saw him as an ugly, fat old man who was no good to anyone. Joe Forrini always felt that women were repulsed by him immediately, and when he could avoid sitting near them in the park, at dinner, or in the movies, he did. Unless they were very old. Then he guessed he did not matter to them one way or the other.

"Is there something wrong?" was what Joe Forrini said to the girl, and the girl—maybe sensing that Joe was someone who wouldn't take advantage of her situation, that Joe, the huge, colorless maverick who stood looking down at her with his apologetic light-blue eyes, would not laugh, or make a pass, or cause a disturbance—the girl, sensing this, told him about it.

She had had a fight with her girl friend, she explained. Her girl friend had moved out of their apartment, and rented a room in Joe's building, across the hall from Joe. Her girl friend was in the room now, with the door bolted. She had a bottle of sleeping pills which she said she was going to take to kill herself.

"That was fifteen minutes ago," the raven-haired girl explained to Joe, "and now she won't answer me. I'm afraid to leave here and go for help. I don't know where I'd go for help. I can't go to the police."

"Why not?" Joe asked. "Do you want me to go?"

"No. Look, this girl is a—she looks like a man." The girl watched Joe's face for some reaction; and seeing none, continued. "Do you know what I mean? People think she is a man. I don't want the police here. Sometimes she's just dramatic. Maybe she's sitting in there right now listening. I don't know. I just don't know what to do."

Joe told the girl that the landlady never allowed bolts on the doors in the building.

"The room key would unlock the door," he said. "Mrs. Donnelly never lets a roomer lock his door with an inside lock."

Joe knocked on the door and called: "Are you there?" There was no answer. He tried the door, but the automatic lock was in place. The black-haired girl began to sob again.

Joe Forrini went down to the landlady's apartment in the basement.

"A friend of mine rented a room across the hall from me," he said. "He's a heavy sleeper, and I'm supposed to wake him up for an appointment, but he doesn't seem to hear my knocking. Could I borrow your passkey to his room?"

The landlady obliged without a moment's hesitation.

Joe and the black-haired girl unlocked the door. There, sprawled out on the bed was the "man-woman," passed out from too much whisky, but very much alive and snoring.

Joe and the girl brought her to. On his electric hot plate
Joe fixed coffee. The girls made up. The trio sat in Joe's room
long past his bedtime. They drank of his wine, and they
laughed with him when he announced that *this* was the most
exciting thing that had happened to him in a long time. The
black-haired girl called him "honey," said over and over how
sweet he was; and the other girl talked man-to-man with him
about a good Chinese laundryman in the neighborhood,
wrestling, and the crazy way the bath down the hall ran cold
water from its hot water faucet and vice-versa.

"Can we invite you to dinner tomorrow night?" the black-
haired girl asked.

Heady with the wine, exhilarated by the friendly conversation, Joe Forrini accepted with pleasure.

The girls wrote down their address and left. It was four
A.M. Joe slept like a baby.

But the next evening, he was Joe Forrini again. He had
already rationalized away his dinner invitation. They just
wanted to return his favor, he decided. They had been drinking too. They really wouldn't want him in their apartment. He
would let them off the hook, and not show up.

When Joe got home at his usual hour, after the Automat
and the park, and the televiewing at the neighborhood bar, the
girls were waiting for him.

"We thought you'd got lost," they said. "Come on; even if
we can't have dinner together, let's have a drink. The drinks are
on us!"

At the entranceway to *Three Flights Up*, the girls told the
husky fellow guarding the door: "He's with us. He's our
friend." *Our friend*, Joe Forrini beamed.

You see Joe with the girls quite often. The girls are Miki
and Morgan. For them, Joe is a very likable guy—someone
they can tease and talk to and have around to the house,
the way they might an older brother or an uncle. They are as

grateful for Joe's friendship as he is for theirs. He's a man they can trust, depend on, confide in, and express their maternal instincts with. He's a friend.

For Joe Forrini, the girls have made a new world, a wider world in which he attains the status of a somebody. At last he finds he can believe he is wanted—just for himself. There is no threat, no feeling of self-effacement or ineffectualness, no ridicule, and most important of all, no loneliness now. Joe has a place to go at Christmas, occasional breaks in his routine, a reason to laugh, to worry, to think, to be—he has two people who care. For the first time in too long for him to remember, the phone on the first floor of the rooming house rings for him now, and less and less does he find the time to complete the crossword puzzle in his newspaper.

Joe Forrini is not a typical member of the Lesbian coterie. Many Lesbians like Miki and Morgan have Joes whom they have met less dramatically, and to whom they may be less devoted. But there is this type always among a certain circle of Manhattan Lesbians. Sometimes he hangs around Lesbians, buys their drinks, listens to their troubles, and seems to find some sort of vicarious pleasure in fraternizing with them. Well into middle age, tired, shy old men buy themselves a seat on the sidelines of this gay game, grateful for the opportunity to watch the minor tragedies and comedies of the Lesbian.

2. Roger . . .

Roger is Olivia's friend. Among male homosexuals, he is considered a "closet queen," one who shys from overt homosexuals in public. Even in private, he is cautious. He never brings a man to his apartment. He prefers to visit the Turkish baths for his sexual expression, or to frequent a subway urinal. He never wants to know his partner's name, or anything about him. He indulges in sex only about once a week, and the time spent takes less than an hour. Roger does not like himself after.

Roger is charmed and excited by men, but not by homosexual men who live a gay life. They disgust him. Lesbians, on the other hand, he considers his best friends. He worships Olivia.

Roger wears a crew cut, and heavy black-framed glasses which he always removes in the company of a man who attracts him. He rarely does anything about such a man, but idolizes him and admires him without overt action. Roger believes "sex" with a man he is fond of would spoil everything.

As hard as Roger claims he tries not to appear effeminate, he is almost a stereotype. His conversation is peppered with such expressions as: "Good heavens!" "Oh, my word!" "I shudder at the very *thought*," and "*Really!*" In discussing ordinary experiences, Roger often uses extravagant adjectives such as "loathsome," "appealing," "divine," and "simply mad!" His exaggerations are made more conspicuous by his habit of placing undue emphasis on certain syllables, and by his acquired tendency to lisp.

A typical conversation of Roger's would run something like this:

"I mean, *honestly*, Olivia, what was I tho think! Time and time again he's pranced in here with those utterly di-*vine* baby-blues and sat himself down opposite me. Really! *Who* does *who* think he's kidding! I cannot abide that type, I mean, I simply *cannot*. Good heavens, he's an *appalling* bore about it tall! I love him dearly, but the boy is simply not *well*, Olivia. I really *must* get him out of my mind!"

Roger is thirty-seven, a blond who uses a hair lightener. He is tall and slender, and justifiably proud of his good male figure in tight, tapered pants. He has an enormous collection of ties and ascots and a penchant for bright red sweaters and socks, as well as for a large variety of after-shave lotions and astringents.

Roger calls all celebrities by their nicknames or their first names. It's Katie this, and Ed that, and Chris, and Noel and Johnny. He reads all the gossip columns, and while he cannot afford very often to dine in the popular, chic clubs about town, he visits all of them for a drink at the bar, which he has an incredible ability to nurse for hours. He does not like gay bars. Roger adores ballet and theater, and usually attends the Saturday afternoon matinees. He is fascinated by antiques.

One of Roger's most consistent topics of conversation is the brutality of heterosexual men. Particularly his father, whom he feels ruined his mother's life. He feels his sister, of whom he is very fond, has had her potentialities arrested by her marriage to a man who thinks of nothing but business. His sister could have been a great musician, he feels, but now she has three children and her life is completely wasted.

Gossip is Roger's favorite pastime; intrigue is the frosting on the cake. He is astounded to hear of the breakup of a well-known Hollywood couple whom he does not know personally as he is to hear of any discord among the gay girls in Olivia's set.

While Roger seems to adore Olivia, Olivia's tendency is to use him as her whipping boy. Because he is not very successful or affluent, most of the time Olivia provides free tickets when she and Tanja and Roger attend theater or ballet or opera together. When the three eat out, Roger pays for himself, but usually accepts a second cocktail on Olivia, or a brandy after dinner. Olivia is prone to remind him of this from time to time.

Roger and Olivia have been friends for well over ten years. Both have weathered one another's emotional storms; and both are completely dependent upon one another. In Olivia's life, women come and go, but Roger stays.

The Rogers in the female homosexual's life in Manhattan are also typical, though limited in their number and their loyalty. Many of them eventually have violent breaks with their

Lesbian friends after a few years—a good many times over the Lesbian's new girl, who might not cotton to Roger. Sometimes there is a series of Rogers in a gay girl's life.

3. Lou and Howie . . .

Lou and Howie live on 13th Street in Greenwich Village. They've been together for two years. Lou is a dress designer, and Howie a teller in a bank. Both boys are in their early thirties; both rather subtle male homosexuals. They visit the gay bars regularly together, and they spend their annual two-week vacation in the summer at Fire Island. But in their appearance, they seem quite masculine, very pink-cheeked and clean-cut, and extremely shoe.

When Lou and Howie give parties they like to have gay girls attend.

"In our apartment building, it looks odd if a lot of men get together for a party. We have windows that face the front, and a lot of snoops on our floor," Howie told me. "We feel better when the girls show up."

Lou and Howie know Cynthia and Jackie Spencer and Connie and Selma.

"We don't see them very often," Jackie Spenser says, "but we go to their parties, ask them by for drinks, and sometimes we all eat together and take in an off-Broadway show."

Lou and Howie are very affectionate with the gay girls. They embrace them, call them "honey" and "doll," and greet them with open arms when they encounter them on the street.

Usually Lous and Howies in the gay girl's life have an ephemeral place, much more ephemeral than a Roger. One reason for this is the obvious one: unlike Roger, Howie and Lou live in the gay male world and have friends from that world. Then, too, they have each other—whereas Roger has no one except Olivia and her set.

Another reason their place in the Lesbian's life is less lasting is the fact that in many instances, their relationships are even more tenuous than the Lesbian's.

But there are usually other Howies and Lous to replace those who drop out of the picture. The girls meet them in bars, in their jobs, and quite often through other girls.

Of course there are many exceptions to these types gay girls mingle with, but generally these three types predominate as the men in their lives.

11.   MY HUSBAND SAYS ...

1. Natalie's Husband . . .

Natalie Griffin's parents had never met Craig. The Griffins arrived in New York late on a Tuesday afternoon, from the small town in Ohio where they lived. At noon Wednesday they were sailing for Europe, a trip both considered daring, educational, and extravagant.

All the way on the train Mrs. Griffin had tittered: "We haven't even seen Texas and here we are on our way to Paris!"

And Mr. Griffin had answered: "Natalo is right! We'll never do it any younger!"

Mrs. Griffin had read and reread Natalie's latest letter as the train sped east. Natalie said she knew they would like Craig; she hoped they were not too disappointed over the elopement, but neither Craig nor she could bear the thought of a big wedding. She cautioned them to let her know when they were sailing, and when they'd arrive in New York! She and Craig wanted to take them on the town.

It had been Mr. Griffin's idea to surprise them.

"After all," he said, "those kids couldn't have much money, and you know Natalo. She'd go out and buy tickets and spend their money foolishly, trying to see that we had fun while we were in the city. Remember, she did that the last time."

Mrs. Griffin remembered. Two years ago, when they had

gone to see her, Natalie did not have a boy friend. She and a rather severely-tailored older woman showed the Griffins the sights. The older woman worked for the same publicity office Natalie worked for, and Mr. Griffin thought she was particularly sullen. He had taken to calling her "sourpuss" in private, between Mrs. Griffin and himself. Both of them had worried a bit over the fact Natalie wasn't meeting eligible men in the city.

"It'll be fun to surprise Natalo," Mr. Griffin had said, "and this way we won't be on the two kids' necks. We'll take them to dinner, and then they can see us off on the boat the next day, and they won't have time to worry about spending their money on tickets, or fixing up their place."

Mrs. Griffin wondered if they ought to call before they took a cab to the address on East 88th, but Mr. Griffin just wanted to see Natalo's face when she opened the door and saw them.

Craig sounded like a nice boy. He was from Florida, and his father was a judge. He had gone to school at Princeton, and he was an art historian who worked for one of the museums.

"'Course I don't know much about Picasso or any of them fellows," Mr. Griffin said, "but at least I don't have sourpuss to contend with this year."

Both Mr. and Mrs. Griffin chuckled, and Mrs. Griffin put her arm in his as the taxi headed up Fifth Avenue.

"Natalie always liked men with brains," Mrs. Griffin said.

Mr. Griffin smiled: "Heck, Mother," he answered, "I'm just surprised one of them fellows could rope Natalo and haul her in. She sure did circles around most of the boys. Wouldn't give them the time of day."

The neighborhood where Natalie lived looked rather shabby, Mrs. Griffin thought, but Mr. Griffin said that was true of a lot of New York neighborhoods.

"This is an old brownstone," he said, leaning forward to pay the cab driver. "Heck, Mother, we can't expect out little girl's husband to be able to afford a palace right off the bat."

"I'm just glad she's happy," Mrs. Griffin said. "She'll be thirty next month. I had a two-year-old child when I was her age."

"She'll have four or five," Mr. Griffin said. "Wait and see, Natalo always does things in a big way, once her mind's made up!"

It was almost six o'clock. The Griffins knew from Natalie's letters, and from their last visit, that Natalie usually got home from the office about quarter to six. She liked to have a cocktail or two before she started thinking about dinner plans. Mr. Griffin had bought a bottle of ready-mixed Manhattans at a liquor store near Grand Central.

"Maybe Craig doesn't drink," Mrs. Griffin remarked as they read the nameplates in the lobby. "Sometimes those studious types don't."

"Natalo wouldn't marry a teetotaler," Mr. Griffin laughed. "No, sir, the man Natalo married can hold his own, you can bet on it!"

The voice over the inter-com was a masculine one. Mr. Griffin held a handkerchief to his mouth to disguise his voice.

"Delivery," he said. "Delivery service."

The voice said something neither of the Griffins could understand, and then Mr. Griffin repeated his words. Eventually the bell which released the lock rang, and admitted them to the building.

They had to walk up three flights, and the halls smelled of cats, and Mrs. Griffin said it looked like a fire trap. Mr. Griffin said the kids had probably fixed up their place real swell, and anyway there was a fire escape out front.

They stood before 4C breathlessly; then Mr. Griffin punched the bell.

A young man answered the door. He wore Bermuda shorts and high socks, and a pink shirt, open three buttons down at the neck. His hair was close-cropped, a too-bright yellow, and he wore a silver medal on a white cord around his well-tanned neck.

"Hi!" he said.

Mr. Griffin beamed. "Craig? Are you Craig?"

The boy said, "No, I'm David. Craig's gone around the corner for some ice. The icebox is broken. Can I do something for you?"

"Is Natalie here?" Mrs. Griffin asked.

"Uh-uh. Haven't seen Nat. Can we give her a message?"

Mr. Griffin cleared his throat. "We're Natalie's parents."

The boy's Adam's apple bobbed and he grimaced. "Well— well, does Natalie expect you?"

"We're surprising her," Mrs. Griffin said. "Will she be home soon?"

"Craig'll be back in a second," the boy said. "Why don't you come in or something?"

The three stood looking at one another.

Then Mr. Griffin stepped past the boy into the apartment, with Mrs. Griffin following gingerly.

Mr. Griffin handed the wrapped package to the boy.

"This ought to go on the ice right away. Is the icebox near?"

"It's broken," the boy said. "Craig's gone for ice. Why don't you sit down."

The Griffins sat on the low couch in the small barren-looking living room. It was very sparsely furnished. There were no rugs on the parquet floor, and no curtains—only straw blinds that were operated on a cord. There were two weird African masks on the wall, and a picture of a sculpture, a male body without a head—a naked body, without a fig leaf. Mrs. Griffin tried not to look at it. There was a hi-fi set with the tubes and turntable exposed, and there was an opera playing. There were two shelves filled with books, and on the Italian marble-topped coffee table was a book on literary criticism and an ashtray filled with cigarette butts, two cocktail glasses, and a half-full pitcher of Martinis.

The boy said again, "My name's David."

He sat down, lit a cigarette and said, "Did you have a nice trip?"

Mrs. Griffin kept staring around the apartment, and Mr. Griffin began stuffing his pipe with tobacco from his pouch.

"Trip was okay," Mr. Griffin said. "Do you know Natalie?"

"Oh, my, yes. Yes, I like Natalie very much. She's a doll!"

Mr. Griffin nodded. Something about the boy's bare knees irritated him, that and the way he crossed his legs so delicately and let one leg swing, watching it as though he greatly admired it.

Mrs. Griffin said, "I'd like to freshen up in the—"

The boy jumped to his feet. "Back here," he said. "Gosh, it's such a mess. We didn't expect company. I'm simply embarrassed."

Mr. Griffin wondered why *he* should be embarrassed.

Mrs. Griffin went in the direction of the bathroom, passing through the bedroom on the way. In the bedroom were two studio couches, pushed far apart. Again, the floors were bare, and there was not much furniture. There was a landscape on the wall, and a potted palm in the corner by a sling chair. She saw a shirt thrown across the chair, and a pair of man's shoes under it. Mrs. Griffin couldn't resist a peek in the closets. One contained a wide variety of suits, shoes, and ties. The other held a few of Natalie's dresses; some heels, and some slacks.

Mrs. Griffin entered the bathroom with the thought that Natalie and Craig might have had a tiff. Maybe Natalie had even gone off somewhere; she was terribly hot-tempered and impulsive.

The bathroom was painted black and gold. It was overloaded with after-shave lotions and men's colognes. Well,

Natalie was never one for perfume. Maybe men in New York used cologne. Times changed, Mrs. Griffin decided, and then she began to worry about Natalie. What if the marriage had gone wrong? But that seemed impossible. Only last week Natalie wrote how happy she and Craig were.

Back in the living room, Mr. Griffin attempted conversation with David. He told Mr. Griffin he was in theater. He designed sets. He thought it was great fun. Mr. Griffin puffed on his pipe and sighed. He supposed young people in New York met all kinds.

Then in the hall, a voice called, "Davie! Open the door! Hey, Davido!"

"Craig," the boy said. "He's back."

Craig stood dumbfounded while the boy introduced Mr. Griffin. Craig was very handsome, a big fellow with a mop of golden hair, a deep tan, and very bright green eyes. Mr. Griffin thought he dressed peculiarly for someone who lives in New York, but David was just as peculiar. Craig wore Italian white pants, made like pajama pants, pulled tight with a cord, and tapered near the ankles. He had on a bright green V-necked blouse, and thong sandals. He wore a silver ring on the little finger of his right hand, and a gold band on his left-hand ring finger.

"I'm simply at a loss for words," he said. "Please—please make yourself comfortable, and let me call Nat."

"Is she still at the office?" Mr. Griffin asked.

"Well, she's with a business associate. Something to do with business. I'm just in a funk, Mr. Griffin. Give me a minute!"

The boy said, "We'll fix you a drink. Craig's got ice."

Mr. Griffin sat back down on the couch and stared across the room at the naked sculpture without the fig leaf.

Mrs. Griffin was washing her hands now, using the bar of perfumed soap, wiping her hands on the black and gold towel with *Craig* emblazoned across it. She could not find a towel with Natalie's name on it. As she opened the door, she heard a voice saying:

". . . got to reach Nat, Jan. Do you know where she is? No, she wasn't home last night. I thought she was with you. Well, good Lord, don't ask *me* where she is? I'm not her keeper! Jan, listen, control yourself. Her parents are here."

Mrs. Griffin caught her breath, and her hands wrapped themselves up in little knots. She did not dare move for fear she would be discovered eavesdropping on the conversation. She could see only the back of the golden-haired boy as he stood in the hallway outside the bedroom, holding the phone in his hands. She saw the wedding ring and thought of his words: *I'm not her keeper*.

". . . well, was she at The Dock last light? Look, Jan," he continued, "this is an emergency. They just walked in on Davy and me! No, nothing like *that*—but we didn't expect them. Good heavens no, they don't know a *thing*!"

Mrs. Griffin held onto the wall. She felt dizzy.

"I'll try Marty's place," Craig was saying then. "Sometimes she stays over with Marty when she's high."

Marty . . . Mrs. Griffin remembered that was "sourpuss's" name.

The phone banged back in its cradle, and before Craig could dial again, Mrs. Griffin rattled the doorknob of the bathroom noisily.

This made the golden-haired boy jump. He whirled and said, "Oh, how do. You must be Nat's mom. I'm Craig."

He came forward, his face flushed, his hand held forward to shake Mrs. Griffin's.

Mrs. Griffin said: "How do you do, Craig."

"This is quite a surprise!" Craig said.

Mrs. Griffin could not think of anything else to say but "I'm very sorry."

Back in the living-room, Davy was saying to Mr. Griffin:

"Oh, Craig is just tip-top in his field. He's a very talented fellow. Really! Ask him anything! I've always said I don't know a brighter fellow than Craig. It's simply appalling how much he's managed to tuck away in that head of his!"

"Don't exaggerate so, Davy!" Craig said from the kitchen.

"He's so modest," Davy told Mr. Griffin. "If I had one speck of his intellect, believe you me *I* wouldn't be modest. It's simply incredible!"

"I'm trying to locate Nat," Craig called in. "Make yourself comfortable. Davy, how about cracking some ice?"

"Roger Dodger." Davy leaped to his feet. "One thing about Craig," he said to the Griffins in a confidential tone, "he's all fingers when it comes to anything like cracking ice." Davy giggled. "All fingers."

Mr. and Mrs. Griffin sat in silence. Craig whisked in, pretending to empty the ashtray, but as he passed the hi-fi, he turned up the opera. "Poor Butterfly" blared in the room. The Griffins were aware of the boys speaking together in frantic tones beyond them in the kitchen.

Mrs. Griffin looked at her husband and said: "Couldn't we go to our hotel and have Natalie call us there when Craig gets a hold of her?"

Mr. Griffin said simply, "Let's!"

The pair rose and went to the kitchen doorway. The two boys jumped apart. They'd been leaning together talking in a nervous, confidential attitude. Mr. Griffin announced that they would be at their hotel.

"Ask Natalie to call us there?" he said.

The hi-fi screamed behind him, and Mrs. Griffin tried to speak above it. "Perhaps we can all have dinner later."

"Is there anyplace we can call Natalie?" Mr. Griffin asked.

"No," Craig said, "but I'll have her call you first thing. The minute I get in touch with her. We were just—unprepared."

"Well," Mr. Griffin said dryly, "we shouldn't have surprised you."

Mrs. Griffin added weakly: "We hope to know you better, Craig."

Again, Craig proffered his hand.

After the door shut behind them, as the Griffins made their way down the stairs, Mrs. Griffin said: "Of course we can't jump to any conclusions until we've talked to Natalie. That's the first thing to bear in mind."

Mr. Griffin didn't answer. . . .

Later that night, Natalie called her parents. They had eaten in their room, waiting for her call, and afterward, they had watched television and flicked through magazines and newspapers. Now and then Mr. Griffin had said: "We shouldn't have surprised them," and Mrs. Griffin had repeated her remark about not jumping to conclusions.

But when Mrs. Griffin heard Natalie's voice, she broke into weeping.

Mr. Griffin took the phone. He said: "Natalo?"

"Daddy?"

"Is everything all right, Natalo? That's what your mother and I want to know?"

"I didn't expect you," his daughter said. "What's wrong with mom? I was at Marty's working on a business problem. What's wrong with Mom?"

"Nothing, big girl. We just want to see you before we go."

"Craig said you were going tomorrow."

"That's right, Natalo."

"We'll come to the boat, Daddy. Craig and I will come to the boat."

"Yes, honey. That would be nice."

"Well, is anything *wrong*?"

"No, we're fine. Are you all right?"

"Daddy, of course!"

"You want to talk with Mother?"

"Well, can she talk? She's all worked up. What's wrong?"

"We were just worried, big girl."

"Look," Natalie Griffin said emphatically, "I'm grown up, Dad! Don't you and Mom realize? I'm not a baby. I'm all grown up! You don't have to worry about me!"

"We're not worried, honey."

"Craig and I will be at the boat, Daddy."

The next day at ten, Craig and Natalie were at the boat. Craig had a bottle of rye and an orchid for Mrs. Griffin, and Natalie kissed them both, and hung on to Craig's arm because she wasn't there yesterday evening.

When the whistle blew Natalie kissed them both again, and Craig shook hands.

The Griffins waved from the deck of the boat until Natalie and Craig were tiny sticks in the distance.

Then, as they sat on the deck waiting for the second sitting at luncheon, Mrs. Griffin said: "I keep remembering that incident in boarding school, when Natalie came home with those letters from that other girl."

Mr. Griffin said he never wanted to hear her say anything like that again. The boat sailed on, and Mr. Griffin turned his eyes from the man across from him, lounging on a deck chair, wearing shorts, and looked toward the sea. He thought of the boy named Davy, and he said: "It's good to be going someplace, isn't it?"

Natalie's husband was saying to Natalie, in a little bar across from the Pier on West 48th: "I don't think they caught on, Nat. Davy's too much sometimes, but he was very careful yesterday. If you'd only let me know where the hell you are, things like this wouldn't happen!"

"It's like Marty said," Natalie Griffin answered. "Parents see only what they want to see. They probably thought we were having a lover's quarrel."

2. Virginia's Husband . . .

"Have a nice day, dear?" Virginia's husband said. He threw his
newspaper on the table in the foyer and dropped his hat on the
chair. He was in his forties. His good tailoring hid the fact he
was too fat. He smoked Upman's and wore garters even when
he was lounging in slacks around the backyard. They had a big
back yard, and a gardener who tended it. The house was in
New Jersey, a forty-five-minute drive from New York. Virginia's husband had a seat on the stock exchange.

Virginia said, "Madge was here."

Virginia was slightly plump herself, but nowhere near fat.
Madge always said she was just lush, and Madge liked lush
women. Virginia was thirty-five. She had been married to
Herbert for ten years. Before she was married, she lived with
her folks down near Deel, New Jersey. Both she and Herbert
were from well-to-do families. Both had known each other
since childhood. Herbert was very staid, and Virginia had
always been more innocent than her years would indicate,
until she met Madge. Madge liked her innocence in the beginning. Madge called Virginia Little Orphan Annie. She said
Virginia had a child's look of bewilderment. They had met
three years ago at a party the matrons in the small New Jersey
town had given for the summer stock players. Madge was an
actress in her middle forties.

"How is Madge?" Herbert asked. "I'm sorry I missed her.
Why didn't she stay on for dinner?"

Even though Herbert's denseness, his absolute lack of
insight, was a boon to Madge and Virginia's relationship, it
always made Virginia slightly disdainful of him when he said
something like that. Here they were—Madge and Virginia—
having a simply mad affair practically under his nose, and he
said, "I'm sorry I missed her. Why didn't she stay for dinner?"

Virginia said, "She had a date in the city for dinner."

"She always seems to come when I'm working," Herbert

said. "Too bad. I like Madge. She has a sense of humor."

It seemed to Virginia that he said that as though a sense of humor were an unusual attribute, but then Herbert had very little sense of humor. Herbert lived for only three things—his work, his yard, and his son. Their son. Herbert was four now, a chubby, bright little youngster who was playing out in the yard with a clay set which Madge had brought him.

Sometimes Madge said, "It makes me nervous to be in here like this with Herbie out in the yard."

"He's been taught always to knock on bedroom doors," Virginia told her. "Besides, he wouldn't notice much."

"Don't kid yourself, Ginny, kids that age are quick."

"Herbie's not. He's like big Herb."

"Sometimes I think you really underestimate your own kid."

"No, I don't. He's a dream, but he's no genius. He's average."

"I love him," Madge said. "And I love you."

"If I didn't have you," Virginia told her, "I'd die on the vine."

"Is he really that bad a lover, baby?"

Virginia said, "He's not a lover. He's just a man who does it once a week, the same way he shaves every morning. Routine."

"Doesn't he know you don't get anything out of it?"

"I don't think Herbert thinks women are supposed to get anything out of it."

"Did you ever think of divorcing him, Ginny?"

"Divorce Herbert? No . . . We're like old shoes."

"And you never fight?"

"Herbert won't fight. That's all there is to it."

Madge would laugh. She would say, "Honestly, this takes the cake. It's all so uncomplicated."

"That's because Herbert's uncomplicated," Virginia would tell her. . . .

Herbert, when he got home, went out and played with Herbie in the yard.

"Aunt Madge was here," Herbie said. "She gave me this."

"That's swell," Herbert said. "Let's build a house."

He sat down on the bench beside the boy, under the trees. This was the time of day he liked best—sunset, when he could return to his family. Herbert considered himself the luckiest man in the world. He had a good wife, a nice kid, stability, all money could buy—really all he ever desired. It couldn't be beat.

When Virginia joined him, bringing their before-dinner sherry on a tray, he leaned back from the clay-building and looked up at her. "You know something?" he said. "I've been thinking more and more about what you said about wanting to take a little vacation."

Virginia had brought the subject up several times. She'd told him she'd just like to go off by herself and relax—just for a week or so. Madge had given her the idea. "We could go to Cuba," Madge had said. "He'd never have to know I was going along. We could meet there. It'd be fun to get away."

It would be wonderful! Madge was exciting and different, and in a way, crazy! Once, in New York, when they met to shop, Madge took her for a ride in a hansom cab through Central Park. It was raining and they were under cover. They'd kissed and clung to one another, and Virginia had thought it was absolutely the craziest thing that had ever happened to her. But then, she had never known anyone like Madge. Before Madge, she had never known any embrace but Herbert's, and that was a cold, embarrassing business. Virginia used to think she was just frigid. Madge said she was one of the most passionate women she had ever known. This frightened Virginia at first, but now it pleased her. Madge was the spice in her life.

Once Madge said, "I've been with more glamorous women than most men have sat next to on a bus, and none of them were Lesbians, either. I don't like Lesbians."

This always made Virginia feel good. Whenever she

thought of herself involved with a woman, she remembered what Madge said, and she never felt that there was anything really wrong about it. Madge said most women who were *real* women had a woman lover in their life.

"I'd love a vacation," Virginia told Herbert, sipping the sherry; "but I hate to leave you alone."

"I think it would be good for you," Herbert said, "but I hate to have you go alone. I'd like to go with you. Yet, it's hard for me to get away right now."

"I know," Virginia said.

Herbert said, "What would you think if I sent you and Madge off somewhere. Say, Bermuda?"

"Oh, Herbert, that's too extravagant."

"No, it isn't. It isn't at all. After all, that way I don't have to worry about some wolf trying to make up to you." Herbert chuckled. "Madge can be chaperone."

"I'd have to ask her," Virginia said. "I don't know whether she would or not."

"We could talk her into it."

"Perhaps," Virginia said.

"Undoubtedly," Herbert said. He smiled. "You know, Madge has done you a lot of good, Virginia. You needed someone like that in your life. Someone peppy. Madge has a good sense of humor."

"I think you're fond of Madge," Virginia said. "Maybe I should be jealous!"

Herbert laughed. "She's hardly *my* type," he said, "I like a more conventional woman."

"Like me," Virginia said.

Herbert nodded. "But it's nice to know a character now and then, isn't it, darling?"

3. Carol's Husband . . .

SUPREME COURT OF THE STATE OF NEW YORK COUNTY OF NEW YORK

CAROL G. SIMON, Plaintiff,
against
DANIEL T. SIMON, Defendant.

STATE OF NEW YORK
COUNTY OF NEW YORK:

I, CAROL G. SIMON, being duly sworn, depose and say:

1. I make this affidavit for temporary alimony, and in reply to the defendant's affidavit sworn to............

2. The defendant's affidavit, dated........................., demonstrates convincingly that in his zealousness to defeat plaintiff's cause of action, he will willingly testify falsely under oath and otherwise trifle with the Court. Thus, while defendant truthfully stated that I was "time and time again at the home of Laura Wedeck overnight" and that this was "with my full knowledge and consent," in his most recent affidavit he states: "My wife saw this woman, Laura Wedeck, behind my back." The defendant, on the one hand, admits he was aware of my close relationship with Laura Wedeck, and on the other, attempts to blacken said relationship by making it appear surreptitious.

3. Regarding p. 36 of the defendant's affidavit, in which he states that I was frank in telling him of my alleged complex history and personal problems, I refer to Exhibit 22, attached to this affidavit, in which defendant declares: " . . . so little I know about you, darling. Won't you confide more in me? No matter what you tell me, I will try to understand. I too have

suffered pain and disappointment. I believe I am shock-proof. Could it be that you fear a homosexual attachment to Laura? Do you think that would make any difference between us? I am your husband, Carol, for better or for worse." It seems obvious that the defendant was more interested in telling me about my personal problems, and equally obvious that I had not confided in him anything.

4. My husband would have the Court believe that my relationship with him was solely without physical involvement during the past two years, that I taunted him by saying I was a man-hater and found men repulsive, and that I also made the statement: "Laura and I can make love all we want, and under the law it is not adultery." This is patently untrue. In Exhibit 32, attached to this affidavit, is his letter which states in part: " . . . you were cold in my embrace. I feel as though I am using you when I make love to you, even though you allow it." This is proof of our physical relationship. Further on in the letter, it is the defendant who states what he claims I states, *i.e.*: "I think sometimes you are trying to drive me to adultery with another woman, while you and Laura can do as you please because under the law it is not adultery."

5. It is true that my husband and I discussed homosexuality on many occasions, as he has stated. However, at no time did I say "I am a Lesbian," as he claims I did, nor did I ever dare him to go out with another woman so I could "take him to the cleaner's and end this morbid marriage once and for all." Whatever excuse my husband may make for his misconduct with the party named, the fact remains he did commit adultery, thus violating our marriage contract.

6. I also deny the charge that I habitually frequented homosexual haunts in Greenwich Village. In the detective's report, it was stated that Laura Wedeck, in the company of another woman, was a visitor at these establishments, but this hardly implicates either Miss Wedeck or me. Miss Wedeck is a

writer who has occasion to visit many places of unusual nature.

7. I, in the interest of preventing the undue protraction of this affidavit, merely reaffirm and reiterate under oath all of the facts contained in my said earlier affidavit. I am certain that these facts will be made clear upon the ultimate trial of this action.

Carol G. Simon

SWORN TO before me this
...............day of ....

12.   A CATERED AFFAIR

"We're celebrating two things," Laura Wedeck said when she made the invitations, "Carol's divorce, and the publication of my new book! It is to be a catered affair, strictly a hen party, this time. We can kick off our heels and relax!"

Laura is between thirty-five and forty, a tall, strong-looking woman with a silver streak in her long black hair. She has large, searching brown eyes, and a small mouth which tips to one side when she talks. She looks like a horse-woman or a golfer; she laughs easily and loudly, with her head thrown back, and she dresses smartly, usually in tweeds or gray flannels or tailored dresses.

Laura is a writer of fact crime, with an occasional children's book tossed in. Before she became a free-lance professional, she was a reporter on a large Midwestern daily. She had been married twice, both times to straight men; both newspapermen. She often says she will marry again one day. Laura considers herself a bi-sexual, but does not believe in mixing both at the same time.

Currently she is involved with Carol Simon. Carol is in her late twenties, a slim, pretty woman who is sullen and neurotic. Carol married Dan Simon to escape from an inner guilt arising from a homosexual attachment in a woman's junior college. Her husband's suspicions of her true nature, and his well-meant attempts to discuss the matter with her, made her more and more belligerent toward him. When he ultimately gave up hope and became involved with another woman, Carol won her divorce case and was granted temporary alimony.

It was not until after the divorce that Carol actually began her relationship with Laura, but certainly their friendship was of a passionate nature, with love spoken and the consummation of that love promised.

The catered affair begins at ten o'clock, with the arrival of the first guests, Tay and Huguette. Laura's apartment is on the West Side, forgivable because it is on Riverside Drive, and the view is a spectacular twelfth-floor one of the river, New Jersey, and the George Washington Bridge.

Laura's apartment has five rooms; a long living room, a large kitchen, two bedrooms, and Laura's study. It is furnished in a traditional style, with many valuable antiques, and a few expensive sixteenth- and seventeenth-century works of art.

The caterers have set the serving table up in the living room, where there are crystal cocktail and highball glasses, canapés and hors d'oeuvres, and a vast assortment of whisky, gin, vodka, and wine. In the kitchen there is ham, roast beef, and turkey for later in the evening, along with cold salads.

While Tay and Huguette take their coats to the bedroom, Laura's agent arrives.

Laura likes to ask her to her parties because "May leads a dull home life, I suspect. She gets a kick out of the gay girls, even though she's straight as an arrow. It's something different for her, poor thing."

May, the agent, always tells her husband: "What I won't put myself through on an evening for ten per cent!"

Janie Allen and Deenie arrive, and Berry and Billy. They've all had dinner together, and too many drinks.

Berry wants to hear a new album on Laura's phonograph, and Janie and Deenie want to dance.

Everyone is dressed in heels and hose, and even though there are two women dancing now, before the others, the party starts off quietly. Laura talks with her agent. Carol, Tay and Huguette discuss a new Broadway play they've all seen. Berry and Billy sit transfixed, listening to "Guess Who I Saw Today."

A few more people arrive, among them Janice, who brings her Siamese cat on a lead. Janice is a sportswear buyer for a large department store. The cat, Speak Up, goes everywhere Janice goes. Janice is one of the Manhattan Lesbians who is always reputed to be having an affair with "a very important woman" who is married. One rarely sees the woman of such a liaison, but Janice claims she is divine, would of course not reveal the woman's name to anyone, and slips away near the end of an evening for a supposed rendezvous.

By eleven o'clock the party is in full swing, more couples dance, more drinks are downed. May, the agent, in a corner alone, waves smoke out of her eyes and pretends to be interested in a paperweight she has picked up off a table. Some of the girls have abandoned their shoes and are dancing in stocking feet. The telephone rings and Laura hears Olivia's voice over the wire:

"I suppose there aren't any men there," Olivia says.

"None were asked."

"Well, darling, look, I'm just in a state. Tanja's gone."

"What do you mean she's gone?"

"She's left me. That's what I mean—left me. She's gotten herself involved with some Village trash, that's what she's done. I think her analysis brought it on; she's gone off with some girl named Kit something or other, and I'm just sick, see?"

Laura says: "I'm sorry."

"So I was wondering if it was all right if Roger came with me. You know Rog. He's a lamb, and he couldn't care less if there are only girls there, and I do need him with me now."

"Bring him," Laura says. "I don't mind."

Carol Simon has joined Laura's agent, in the corner.

Carol always talks as though she were not one of the gay crowd, as if to prove to an observer that this was not her milieu at all.

"My husband," she says, "always wanted to be a writer too. But he never had much success. He was quite clever—more like an English writer, a Waugh or a Greene."

May, however, is not fooled. She has bought too many cocktails for Laura before lunch, and too many brandies after, and heard too many times Laura's complainings: ". . . so I simply won't let anything happen between us until Carol gets her divorce. No matter how much she wants it to happen I have a conscience. And the whole thing is tearing me apart inside, May. That's why my work is slowing up. I just can't think of another thing but Carol and me."

Carol continues: "Of course, we're divorced now, but the next man I marry better not aspire to being a writer. I just can't compete with that!"

There is always a Carol among the gay crowd. She's the little girl who isn't there—the one who can never reconcile her way of life with other people's opinions of that way of life. She feels obliged to discredit her homosexual sisters by pretending to appear removed from their plight.

"Many of the girls here," she tells May, "are really very interesting, despite their peculiarities."

On the street, she is always quick to correct Laura, should Laura take her arm under an umbrella, or call her attention to something in a store window by touching her.

"Don't be so obvious!" is her reproach.

Yet their most serious arguments stem from the fact that Laura refuses to say that she was not happy with her former husbands; refuses to say, as Carol says: "Men are repulsive to me sexually."

Olivia and Roger arrive with a great squeal from Roger: "Oh, good heavens!"

Roger, it develops, is sensitive to cats. They give him asthma. Janice flees toward the bedroom with Speak Up.

"Just shut the door and leave him in there," Laura says. "He'll be all right!" To Roger she says, "You know, there's an interesting fellow across the way—a gay fellow who does musical arrangements. I've always thought of asking him over one night. Maybe I should now."

"Don't go out of your way," Roger answers.

But Laura doesn't understand that Roger means it; that Roger does not like other gay men. She promptly starts out the door.

Tay listens to Olivia sympathetically: ". . . and that was that, Tay. She just walked out on me. Went off with this Village creep named Kit!"

Roger says: "And after all Olly did for her, the little tramp. Paying for her analysis and giving her the show and everything. I was really seething inside when I heard about it. Seething!"

There is a piano in the corner by the window, and Olivia steers Roger toward it. "C'mon, Rog," she says, "Mama's got to lose the blues. It was that analyst that did it, the goddam headshrinker. Told her she was a goddam masochist, you know. Said she was a masochist!"

While Roger plays old show tunes and sings, Laura returns with Andrius, the man across the hall.

Andrius looks like a little boy. He is short and slim and delicate. His hair is cropped close but combed forward in front, in a bangs effect. He wears a suit with an Edwardian cut, a bright red vest, and a white carnation in his buttonhole.

"I just this second got in the door," he says to Laura.

"That's Roger over there playing the piano. I didn't want him to be the only male."

Andrius glances at him. "Isn't she a little old for me?" he says.

"I don't know." Laura laughs. "Is she?"

Andrius is the gay of the gay, the kind who perpetually "camps." Men are "she's" and women "he's." Andrius is a poser from his forehead to his toes, a straight-faced comedian of gay patter, with the slight lisp, the arched eyebrow, and the certain tilt to the head that are the accompanying dressing. Andrius pokes his head into a circle where Deenie, Janie Allen, Berry and Billy are talking.

He says, "Owwww, she's so pret-ty!"

"Who is?" Janie Allen asks.

Andrius says: "*I* am!"

Now Laura brings the food from the kitchen, and the guests cue up for plates and silverware.

We hear Tay, in line, saying to Huguette: "Well, Olivia's better off without Tanja. She was a little kid who was nowhere!"

Huguette says: "That Andrius, he is funny, ah?"

Carol Simon is telling May: "Of course, when I have children, I'm not going to force any religion down their throats. The next man I marry—"

Janice is saying: ". . . because she's someone who just can't afford scandal! I've never loved anyone so deeply in my life. Of course, it's terrible the way we have to sneak around . . ."

Roger comments to Olivia, "I certainly don't want to believe that Laura would *dream* I'd even want to *shake hands* with that loathsome queen she brought from across the hall!"

And Olivia, not listening, is saying to Roger: "Maybe if we went down to The Dock, Tanja'd be there! I'm not going to chase after her, God damn it, but in a way I blame myself, because I got her involved with that head-shrinker."

The catered affair—not too different from many catered affairs. It is sumptuous and merry and smoky and getting a little drunk, and as it nears its burnt-out end and forces its imminent crises, guests go for coats, stay for *one* more, promise to call someone they haven't seen in a long time, stare with bewilderment at the cigarette hole in their dress wondering how that got there, replenish their make-up in the bathroom, notice a pair kissing in the shadows off by the hall closet, and say "Everything was wonderful, really. Really wonderful!"

Janice's words come from the bedroom: "My God, Speak Up, you've eaten a hole in one of Laura's cashmere sweaters!"

And Andrius' words sound in the hall by the closet: Huguette, you are a sweet child, but what possible fatal attraction could you have for little old me! Now your girl friend's going to be peeved, pet, and Andrius doesn't want to fight him, love!"

Olivia says, "Rog, I'm asking you to do this as a favor. We won't *stay*! I just want to walk into The Dock and *see*! Now, Rog, I've done a hell of a lot for you!"

Carol says, in the living room: "Of course, I don't really believe in alimony, but Dan *was* unfaithful, May, and after all, he did take up some of my best years!"

Tay's words come from the kitchen: "I think that faggot you asked over, that neighbor of yours, Laura, I think he's really a goddam Lesbian in his heart. He's been all night making up to Huguette!"

And random words come from a phonograph record playing over and over because no one listens now:

   . . . guess who I saw today, my darling,
   I saw you . . .

If Olivia had been able to talk Roger into taking her to The Dock that evening after Laura Wedeck's party, she would have just missed Tanja, but she might well have overheard the following conversation among two of the girls at the bar.

"Wasn't that Kit who just left?" one said.

"Yes."

"Was she with that girl?"

"They just started going together."

"I thought Kit went with Eve Cudahy."

"No, Eve left her to go with Betty Rodale."

"Really! I thought Betty went with Judy."

"Judy and Grace have been together ever since that summer on Fire Island when Olivia left Judy."

"Oh. Well, who does Olivia go with?"

"No one now. Tanja just left her."

"Tanja?"

"The girl who just left with Kit."

Hands-Around, the most often played game among Manhattan Lesbians, keeps the jewelers busy engraving new sentiments on watches, bracelets, coins and rings; keeps landlords busy changing the nameplates in the vestibules of apartment buildings; keeps the post office busy with change-of-address cards; the phone company busy with new listings, and the moving men busy moving one girl's belongings out of one apartment and into another.

A gay boy I know put it this way:

"The Lesbians are always criticizing us because of our one- and two-night stands. They pride themselves on the fact they stay together for a year or two. All I can says is, they're playing the same we are, only they stretch out their innings. At least when we break up, we don't trouble the whole damn town about it!"

Lesbians, in their youth, play Hands-Around much more frequently and much more frantically than do those approaching their middle or late thirties. Intrigues thrive at a variety of levels.

First, of course, there is the obvious intrigue of a new change of partners. Two girls I know who recently did a switch and ended up together, told me that they couldn't wait to go to dinner at the Dunes on the following Friday night.

The Dunes, unlike The Dock or Three Flights Up, is a favorite dinner spot for gay girls. While the Dunes caters for the most part to a normal crowd, the girls eat there with regularity. They dress to go there and eat.

At The Dock the gay girl does not feel out of place in pants or Bermuda shorts. The Dock is more of a favorite among the "circle in the square," while the Dunes is favored by the uptown clique who come to the Village for a late dinner.

The two girls I just mentioned told me:

"Wait until everyone sees us walk in together! That'll be the last straw. No one ever thought we'd get together!"

There *is* considerable delight in anticipating what everyone will think when a new pair begin to go together. When this wears off, it is replaced by the delight taken in anticipating what everyone will think when a new pair seem to *stay* together. Lesbians, like mothers of newborn babies, get accustomed to reckoning time by months instead of years. They say,

"We've been together seven months now," instead of half a year, or, "We've been together thirteen months now," instead of a little over a year.

Another aspect of the intrigue involved in the game of Hands-Around is that of social climbing, or nest hunting. On the one hand there is a type like Kit, who took Tanja away from her good provider, and from her social environment, and automatically demoted her to a Village status. Kit then has won some certain victory over the uptown clique, to her mind. Among her colleagues she is looked upon with considerable respect.

More commonly, however, the girl who inveigles the more successful girl, and climbs up the ladder, instead of pulling others down to her level, is deserving of more plaudits.

One such girl was described this way by a former friend: "I can remember Dibby when she was a broke little part-time waitress, who owed everyone in the Village money. When she paid anyone by check, the check bounced before the ink was dry. She used to have every known form of bill collector in New York City on her doorstep, and her doorstep was always someone else's. She is a parasite. Well, now, five years later she still is, but she's a respectable one. She goes with Helen Rollei, the stage manager. Helen made her her assistant, and taught her everything she ever needs to know about the business. Soon she'll be a union member, and she'll never have to worry about getting a job even if Helen and she break up. Meanwhile she lives high off the hog. Helen feeds her, clothes her, and pays her a salary, buys her stock, and has a will made out with her as benefactor. She's a long way from Greenwich Village and waiting on tables these days."

Many times among Lesbians it is well understood that romance, or the love relationship, is far in the background as the basis for two girls' becoming involved. The same girl who described Dibby's present status said to me:

"I offered to give Dibby the moon once, before she was going with Helen. Of course, I didn't have the moon to give. That was the problem. At the time I was still an assistant editor, the next thing to a secretary. Dibby was just starting to get interested in Florence Dee, and Florence had an inherited income—big house, no financial worries, the works. Dibby naturally chose Florence."

Another girl, explaining a breakup of a relationship which had lasted for three and a half years, never touched on a romantic disenchantment as the reason for losing her girl friend, Vivian.

She said: "Diana Houseman came along with her mink coats and her Austin-Healy and her Doberman pinschers and took Viv off. What could I do against that kind of competition?"

The following is a typical conversation between two friends who have met after some time, and are comparing notes.

"Who are you going with now?"

"Jill Locke."

"Who's she?"

"She went with Elizabeth Arch, the choreographer."

"No kidding! The one with the big beach house in Southampton?"

"That's right."

"Didn't she do the choreography for *Tell The Boys* last fall?"

"That's right. And for *The Golden Promise*."

"Sure, I know Elizabeth Arch. I don't know her, but I've certainly heard of her. Isn't she the one who owns that house down on the Mews in the Village?"

"Yes."

"Oh, she's supposed to be a real riot! I've heard she's a ball!"

"She hangs around with a very flashy set, all theater."

"That's what I've heard."

"Europe every summer and all that."

"That's what I've heard."

"Jill tells fabulous stories about her."

"Who does?"

"Jill. The girl I'm going with now."

"Oh, yes . . . Yes, I've heard of Elizabeth Arch. Who hasn't!"

"Everybody, I guess."

"Well, I'm so happy for you. It sounds divine!"

It can be taken for granted that the story will be passed on this way:

"I met Beth on the street the other day, and she told me the most divine news. She's going with a girl who used to go with none other than Elizabeth Arch!"

A Lesbian I know was moved to express the phenomenon of Hands-Around in the following verse, entitled "The Girl I'm Going With Now."

I'm going with Jane,
Who went with Jean,
The girl who was a beauty queen,
Who went with Lee,
Who had the house,
She got from Bee,
Who goes with Krauss,
Who just broke off,
With Helen Roth,
The girl from Maine,
Who went with Jane,
Before she went with Jean.

14.   OLD SOLDIERS NEVER DIE

1. Tockie . . .

Tockie is sixty-two. The only time in her life she ever wore a dress was between her birth and early adolescence, when her family dressed her for church or for a special occasion. Otherwise, as a youngster, Tockie wore her other brothers' hand-me-downs.

Tockie, in her own eyes and in her family's eyes, was a boy. Her brothers teased her, calling her their little kid brother. Her immigrant father was proud of the way Tockie worked on the farm. Her mother was glad Tockie worked on the farm. Her mother was glad Tockie didn't fool around with fellows the way some girls did. Tockie led a relatively happy existence as a youngster and throughout her early teens.

When she was sixteen, it got rough. The kids at school began to make fun of her. The teacher wrote demanding that Tockie appear in female garb. Tockie's older brother, whom she worshipped more than any other member of the family, said one day to Tockie:

"There is such a thing as a queer. You better wear dresses and let your hair grow long or you'll be one of them."

At sixteen, Tockie ran away from home and wandered to Los Angeles. She worked in a shipping room for a while, until it was discovered she was a girl. Then she worked in a bowling alley, setting up pins, and she fell in love with a girl who worked at a counter in a luncheonette across the street. Unwittingly the girl went out with Tockie a few times. One night, on a park bench, the girl's hand wandered across Tockie's shirt in a display of affection, and to her horror, the girl discovered Tockie's breasts. The counter girl quickly spread the story about Tockie, and once again Tockie was forced to quit her job.

She worked here for a week, and there for another, and a year passed before she found out she was not alone in this world, not a freak apart from all other human beings. On the advice of a sympathetic cab driver, Tockie got a job as a waiter in a gay club on The Strip. Then Tockie was launched as a full-blown member of transvestite society. . . .

Tockie's life was a series of jobs in gay clubs all over the United States—San Francisco, Detroit, Chicago, Miami, Atlantic City, Grand Rapids and New York.

Tockie always worked for her living. She prided herself on that. She was not like some of those who lived off their girls.

Tockie had many, many girls. She was handsome and quick and confident, and she never had to cruise a girl she wanted very long.

In 1922, Tockie came to work in New York City permanently. She worked in a Manhattan speakeasy, and lived down in Greenwich Village when that area was at its height in various expressions of Bohemianism. Tockie was thirty-seven, then, handsome and fearless and proud of her success with women. The song that year was "Ain't We Got Fun." *Babbit* was poking fun at American small-town life. Flappers were everywhere, and Edna St. Vincent Millay had already popularized the thought of burning one's candle at both ends.

Tockie fell in love with the spirit of things, and Tockie also fell deeply in love. Her girl's name was Millie, a beautiful titian-haired showgirl who always picked Tockie up in a certain restaurant in the Village when she finished work. Tockie worked days then, and nights waited for Millie to be through work.

Tockie was true to Millie in her fashion, but her fashion was somewhat wayward. Those evenings while she was waiting for Millie, she began to notice the women around her. Gradually she began to take the women for visits to the apartment she shared with Millie. It was said that Tockie could walk in and then walk out with any woman in the place. No man could compete. Tockie was a spectacular figure, big, handsome, with a sure swagger and a winning smile. She wore clothes well, and her confidence was phenomenal.

Aware of this was a small band of neighborhood boys in their late teens. One night, they decided to "get" Tockie. As she started for the restaurant, they overpowered her, dragged her into an alley, and beat Tockie blind and senseless.

Tockie's boss, a few friends, and a brokenhearted Millie helped with the medical bills, and supported her while she was attempting recovery. But Tockie never saw again, and never got quite well mentally. After a while, Millie married and moved to Michigan.

Still living in the Village, Tockie assists a newsdealer on a corner. She looks for all the world like an old man as she walks along with her police dog, dressed in her cap and jacket and pants.

2. Nan . . .

Nan is fifty-seven, a plump, bespectacled music instructor at a small junior college in Vermont. She is a pleasant, cheerful woman, loved by her students. There are still traces of her quiet beauty, and there are a vast amount of stories circulated by the girls about her "loves." Some say she loved a Frenchman who was already married—because of her melancholy descriptions of Paris when she was there. Others say she loved a man who was killed in the war. Others that she loved a famous musician, who did not reciprocate. All agree that it is a shame Miss Nan was never married; all think of her as a rather mysterious and wonderful woman, who has an ability to give meaning to music which they had never appreciated before taking her classes.

Miss Nan did indeed have a great love affair, but it was not with a man, and it did not come about until she was thirty-eight years old.

During her youth, she was a shy, serious girl, dominated by a mother who was determined to make a concert pianist of her. When she was not practicing and performing for civic groups in the small town in upstate New York where she lived, she was doing her schoolwork, or resting—but very seldom enjoying the companionship of others her age.

In college, she was a good student, but a bad mixer. Her colleagues were bewildered by her alarming enthusiasm for music, and by her incredible inability to talk small talk. The one or two young men who tried to interest Nan were discouraged by her silences, her obvious nervousness, and her embarrassing self-consciousness in their presence.

Nan took graduate work, and, as always, outside instruction in piano and violin. She returned home at twenty-seven, to teach in the local high school, and to live with her mother, who was aging now, and ill.

For her years, Nan acted and appeared much older than she was. Those in the small upstate community already considered her a rather pathetic, withdrawn spinster. Her mother had given up the dream of ever seeing her daughter become a famous concert pianist, but she did not give up nagging at Nan about her failure to become successful.

For years, Nan taught at the high school, performed for P.T.A. meetings and Rotary and Elks and the Community Chest, and continued to care for her mother.

Love was something she understood only vicariously—through her music. It was something she dreamed of, the way a pauper dreams of riches, as though it were glorious and impossible, and only meant for dreams. . . .

In 1937, Nan's mother died. Alone for the first time in her life, feeling no consolation in the town where she lived, Nan decided to go somewhere where no one knew her. Perhaps she could be different then; perhaps, make friends, laugh, find some identity in some new, less familiar microcosm. She applied for a job as a music instructor in a small boarding school for girls in Virginia.

There, in the beginning, things were not too different. She found it difficult to be the new person she had thought she could become. She was not used to loosening up around people, and she had trouble getting to know the other faculty members. She was fond of her students, but she was not able somehow to communicate this feeling to them. She knew that they thought of her as a rather prissy, colorless woman who was much older than thirty-seven. Her music was her saving grace. Few could fail to thrill to the emotional impact of her performances; few could help but wonder how this woman could bring music alive in so stirring a manner.

Then a new faculty member came to assist Nan in the music department. She was in her late twenties, a refugee from Hitler's Nazi Germany, a lovely, equally shy girl whose name was Adele.

In Munich, Adele had been a famous concert pianist. Like Nan, her life had been music—but unlike Nan, she had known a certain bond of gaiety and love within the family group, all members of whom were musicians like herself. She had had a boy friend who was a composer, but their romance had been a mild one, unpassionate and more like a friendship. She too had dreamed of a greater love—the sort of love her music spoke to her about.

Adele and Nan found that love together. For both, it was a sudden joy, a grand, shocking electric impulse that ignited them and kept them in constant wonder at it. They became inseparable. Their affair was untainted by rumors or suspicions or criticism. The other faculty members thought it was fine that Nan had found a friend who could appreciate and share her interest in music; and they were also gratified to see Adele adjust in a world away from her imprisoned family and the memories of being a Jew under Hitler. The students thought Nan did more to make herself attractive, and they too, were not untouched by Nan's kindness to this woman who was a symbol of the persecution and cruelty they had been learning about in their modern history classes.

Everyone in that boarding school sat transfixed at the dual piano concerts when Nan and Adele played together— Beethoven, Chopin, Rachmaninoff, resounded in the assembly hall, and these two women seemed to make a magic.

During the summer, Adele and Nan went to Paris to study and live, and in the fall, they returned to school for another idyllic year. Another summer, and another year passed, and finally in 1940, both women left the school to take jobs in New York City.

They furnished their own apartment, attended all the wonderful concerts New York offers, and taught at separate schools. They made mutual friends, men and women, and their life together was full and busy and never without that breathtaking awareness of the love they shared.

Adele gradually gave up teaching and devoted her full time to re-establishing her career as a concert pianist. Finally, in 1943, she was asked to join a group going to entertain overseas. This was something she could not, and would not *want* to refuse to do. Nan would keep the apartment and wait for her return. It was a tearful parting, and its aftermath was showered with letters back and forth, reaffirming their love, planning their future together. At the end of 1943, Adele was killed somewhere in Italy in a jeep accident.

It is fourteen years since that happened. Nan never fell in love again. But those six years she had of love tell in little ways—a certain look her students say they see in her eyes when she is listening to music, a seemingly sad nostalgia she communicates whenever she talks about Paris, and a certain empathetic understanding she has of their love-restless quandaries. In one big way too, those six years of love tell. There are persistent rumors in the small junior college that Miss Nan can play piano like a professional. Yet she has never touched the keys.

Elaine and Polly . . .

At thirty-eight, Polly was afraid. She had just broken off with a girl she had lived with for three years. Prior to that time, she had lived with many girls, and had many breakups, but suddenly the future looked darker than it ever had. She was tired of the ephemeralness of gay life. She was thinking of herself ten years from 38, when she would be approaching 50. What would she have to show for this life of defiance against the norm? Who would she have whom she could truly count on once she was old? What if she were alone? Sick? Who could she turn to?

Polly was a bookkeeper in a publishing house then. She had always wanted to be an actress, but somehow she had never really applied herself, never really given everything she could to that ambition. She had walk-on parts in Broadway shows, and she had done summer stock, but somehow in her twenties and thirties, she had done those things a serious aspirant actress could not afford to. She had drunk too much, stayed out too late, spent too much money so that she had to take too many full time jobs, and she had exhausted too much energy in the ups and downs of her various affairs.

She could not count on her family. There was only her mother, barely managing to live on her father's insurance, and a brother with a large family of his own. She would not want to ever have to live with either, in any case.

At age 38, Polly had lost contact with many of her crowd—the gay girls she used to know and hang around with. Some of them had moved out of New York; others seemed now to be going out less; a few had even married and some were as unhappy and depressed as she was, which made her all the more aware of her own anxieties.

Elaine was 36. She had moved to New York to take a job as a research librarian. She was from Los Angeles, and the girl she had been living with, a very young girl in her early twenties, had decided to get married and have a family, and escape from gay life. Elaine too, was disenchanted with her life. She vowed never to get mixed up with a woman again. One or two evenings a week she had dinner with a Mr. Palmer, a bachelor in his fifties who wrote books about butterflys, and taught courses in biology at a New York prep school. They had met in the library where Elaine was employed.

Elaine's family lived back in Los Angeles, but they had never approved of her. Aware of her homosexuality, they had told her she was welcome home "anytime she changed."

Polly really had no type.

Mr. Palmer had met Polly one day when he had had to wait to see his publisher. He had waited in the room where Polly worked, and they had struck up a conversation which was pleasant and moved fast. Mr. Palmer thought it would be nice if Polly and Elaine met, because he knew Elaine had few friends in New York. He asked Polly if she would feel he was presumptuous if he were to ask her for drinks one evening at his apartment.

Polly and Elaine liked one another immediately. After their initial meeting they saw a lot of one another. They confided their mutual disenchantment with the gay life, and they said over and over again that it was wonderful to know each other as friends.

Mr. Palmer, Polly and Elaine became a threesome. They ate dinner together, went to theaters together, and went on weekend jaunts to the beach together.

One night when they were on one of their weekend jaunts, after Mr. Palmer turned in, Polly and Elaine had a few nightcaps. A little high, they made love. There were no rockets set off, no stars falling, no particular electricity—but there was mutual enjoyment. They made a joke about the possibility of their ever falling in love with one another.

After that night, there were others like it.

Polly and Elaine began to depend on each other, to find no one else became more important in their lives than the other.

When a year had passed, the girls decided to live together. This affair, both agreed, would be different—because it was not really an affair. They were not in love. No one would be hurt. They would be less lonely, and neither one, they both agreed, was interested in a love affair in the future.

Polly and Elaine have lived together for 12 years now. It is very likely they will live together for many, many more years. They share a bank account, are each others beneficiaries, own a car together, and a small beach cottage at Point Lookout. They celebrate the anniversary of their moving in together, and in every other way, live much as married folk—even sharing the support of a child, under the Foster Parents Plan.

Occasionally they make a joke about the possibility of their ever falling out of love with one another.

15.   DEAR ANN ALDRICH

What kind of mail does the author of a gay book receive?
How much mail does such an author receive?
What kind of people write such an author?
What kind of letters do these people write?

As a result of my first book *We Walk Alone* I have received to date well over 600 letters. The majority are from women, though a good percentage are from men. These letters are a testament to the fact that homosexuality is a subject about which people are not simply morbidly curious, or peculiarly titillated, but a subject about which the average person is either uninformed or misinformed, and about which the troubled person is deeply anxious, distressed and concerned.

Edmund Bergler, writing in *Homosexuality: Disease Or Way of Life?* speaks out against the present policy followed by newspapers and magazines in which there is "a conspiracy of silence" on the topic of homosexuality.

Caprio, in *Female Homosexuality*, states that only by presenting the true facts about homosexuality can we hope to deal with it intelligently, and keep it from becoming a serious sociological disease.

Dr. George W. Henry in his introduction to his study *Sex Variants* writes: "I am aware that there are few topics of which arouse personal feelings as quickly as that of sexual maladjustment. I would like to believe that this subject could be considered as objectively as other medical problems . . ."

So long as there is this "iron curtain" attitude toward the subject of homosexuality, so long in time is a solution to this problem forthcoming.

D.J. West, writing in *The Other Man* says: ". . . those responsible for training children, administering the law or advising on public morals cannot fulfil their duty to the community if they keep themselves in ignorance of certain facts. Homosexuality is a part of life that intelligent people should know about and understand. Unhealthy ignorance causes an almost unbelievable amount of misery and frustration."

Let these letters quoted here be a testament to a more appalling fact than that of people's obvious misery and frustration—to the fact that on so serious a subject as homosexuality there is no one to turn to but a person whose name one copies down from the cover of a book on that subject.

The names have been changed, the cities omitted. The letters speak for themselves.

From a small town in Indiana:

> Dear Ann Aldrich:
>
> This is a very small chance, but we have read your book and we are wondering if you could help us?
>
> We have a daughter who has what we call a crush on her math teacher, a woman. We think the math teacher mentioned is one of those you wrote about. We have always thought so, and we have friends who think the same opinion. She is very much like the woman in THE WELL OF LONELINESS, a mannish type.
>
> We do not want to have this woman fired as we may be wrong entirely, but what if we are not wrong?

Our daughter has in the back of one of her books a heart with an arrow and this woman's initials. She likes to wear blue jeans and shirts when she comes home from school, but we do not let her as we do not want to encourage her to be like a man.

We would die if she were to turn out a lesbian and it would kill my husband, as she is our only child.

Do you think we should tell her to stop this business or is this a stage?

Any thoughts on the subject are welcome from you as this is driving us crazy.

Thanking You,
Mrs. J.T.

From a suburb of Washington, D.C., a letter in part:

. . . I don't know who or what you are, Ann Aldrich, but I feel that someone, anyway, can hear my pourings out. Everything I have told you about my boss, and my losing my job is true, you can believe me, and now even though I don't have much hope, I feel better because I can talk to someone. I never asked to be what I am. I hate what I am. But here I am—me. I don't know where to go from here.

At one time I would have felt I could not sign my name, but now I am so shamed anyway, what does it matter? Will you answer me? Is there someway I can see a doctor you could give me the name of who could change me?

In any event, I will be waiting for a reply from you, please!

Sincerely,
Jane B.

From a city near Chicago, a letter in part:

I am not foolish enough to demand a life of unrelieved jollity. But I am young and healthy and generally good humored, and I think if people, in whatsoever condition or development, can't wonder at beauty, love something, and laugh at the world from time to time, they are wretched indeed. And if they can't, when need be, laugh at themselves, they are lost. It seems to me, further, that most people encourage these aptitudes, either in self defense or for the sake of their sanity, and I will cheer them on at it from nonage to dotage.

To my knowledge, I have never fallen in love, except with music and intelligence; not my own, for its limitations are woefully manifest, but with any mind and talent that can command mine. I can't analyze my curiosity about your book (that is, I would be afraid to), but I don't suppose it qualifies me for anything. However, if it elicits a letter from you, Miss Aldrich, it will at least have an acceptable raison d'être, by which I fear I mean one I can rationalize.

Thanks so much for your time and attention . . . and for your book.

Sincerely,
Mary Ellen L.

From a small town in upstate New York:

Dear Ann Aldrich,

I hope you will not laugh at me for what I am going to say.

I am a man who is laughed at here in the city because I walk and talk like a sissy.

There is nothing I have been able to do all my life to be different. It is true I do not like women in the way a man should. They always leave me cold. But I am not a sissy who likes other men.

Always I get laughed at and it is this ridicule that is making me so miserable, Miss Aldrich, and I am wondering if you could tell me the name of a lesbian I can marry. That would stop the talking behind my back.

I have a good job, am a body-fender and repair man, and I am not old, but in my thirties. Not bad to look at.

I would be a good husband, too, and give a wife what she wanted, and she would not have to expect me to be a man to bother her in any way physical, as I am not interested in that. Believe me I would give her a good home and what she wanted.

There must be someone who would not mind this. I am so desperate for help, and I know if I was to marry, no one would think what they think anymore. Please tell me if you know such a woman, or if you would be interested yourself.

Thank you, and write soon,
Ted L.

From Pennsylvania:

Dear Ann Aldrich,

I read your book with interest, but I disagree with you.

I would like you to write me answers to the following questions.

1. You say a Lesbian can be cured, but she needs to see a doctor. Why can't a man who knows how to understand her problem cure her? Isn't patience, and

sympathy on the part of such a man more important than a doctor's giving advice?

2. Why didn't you get cured?

3. Wouldn't a baby cure a Lesbian? Once she settled down with her own baby and a husband, wouldn't she forget all that?

4. Aren't there only certain kinds of doctors who will cure this? Not any doctor will!

5. You say a Lesbian has to want to be cured! How does she know if she's never tried?

My girl friend is a Lesbian but we plan to get married anyway.

I gave her your book to read, and she says there are no doctors here in . . . . who would be able to help her. I say she doesn't need to go to one. The girl she loves is married, but she will not see her anymore, so what difference can a doctor make?

I bet you won't reply to this letter. But I would be glad if you did.

Your truly,
Jack W.

From New York City:

Dear Ann Aldrich:

You blame the parents for it all, and you have some nerve!

My daughter never listened to me once when I told her she was turning into a freak! She just went on her merry way and did as she pleased! She went out with these rough girls and tried to imitate them, and when I locked up her clothes, all those slacks and shirts, she ran off from home. Then she had the nerve to return after some months.

Why don't you write a chapter about the shame the parents are put through when their daughters act like Lesbians. Time and time again my neighbors said things like well, I see . . . . is with that girl all the time with their arms wrapped around each other, and what did I have to say to them?

I just thank God I have a girl who is normal and decent and is going to marry a nice boy in June. I can be proud of her, and hold my head up, but . . . . is my disgrace. I tell her that and she says I don't want to understand her. What kind of talk is that from someone who doesn't give two hoots what anyone thinks or how humiliating it is to me to see her a queer!

Oh no, Ann Aldrich, it is not the parents who are to blame, but these kids who don't have respect for their parents who raised them, and think they can get away with murder!

Stop blaming the parents for things like this!

Sincerely,
Mrs. W.Y.

From New Hampshire:

Dear Ann Aldrich,

I am not one who writes letters very often, but after reading *We Walk Alone*, I decided to break this rule.

I live in a small town where everyone knows everyone else's business. I am very fond (I think you might say I am in love with her) of a woman in this town who is married. You see, she is like a mother to me. By that I mean, she is kind and goes out of her way to be nice to me, a thing my mother does not bother with. My mother likes my brothers, but she is not good to me. My father is all right and takes up for me, but what I miss is a woman who cares for me. My mother never has put her arms around me or kissed me or said she loved me, not once in my life.

This woman I mention calls me Honey and hugs me, and treats me like a daughter. She has no children and she is about thirty.

I am sixteen now, and this woman is my whole life. My mother runs her down and says she is a snob, but Miss Aldrich, she is one of the sweetest, most wonderful persons in the whole world. Even my father says she is nicer to me than my mother is.

My problem is this. I am happy now but it is only because of this woman. I do not like the boys at High, and I have few close girl friends, and those I have are silly. I like to read poetry and this woman reads poems to me sometimes, and I write poetry about her, but not to her knowledge. What worries me is what is going to become of me as I grow older? I do not want to be a Lesbian. I know I would be very unhappy if I could not get married and be normal, but I cannot seem to get my mind off this woman. I think of her all the time, and sometimes when her car is parked on the main street in town, I sit in it and wait for her for hours to return.

I guess you might say that I am obsessed.

There is no one I can talk to about this problem, because . . . . is so small, everyone knows everyone else's business. I am worried about becoming a Lesbian. Do you think there is a chance I will grow up and forget this woman eventually? Even to think of such a thing is a terrible thing to imagine. But what else can happen to me?

I think I'm not a Lesbian now, because what you wrote about them kissing and the other stuff, made me feel disgusted, but what if I change into one because of the way I am heading?

When you write to me, I do not want you to write to me at my home, because my mother is a terrible snoop, and I am afraid she'd find out. Write to me ? . . . . at . . . . and I will receive the letter safely. That is the address of the woman. I know I can trust her not to open my mail or try to read it, and I have told her I have a friend who will write to me at her home.

Please, please answer and tell me your thoughts about me, and do not be afraid to be frank and honest, as I can take it.

Thank you for reading my letter. I will look forward to hearing from you very soon.

Very truly yours,
Virginia H.

From California:

Dear Miss Aldrich:

I am a girl who is a Lesbian.

I am trying to stop being one. I have had three girl friends in my life, but I am not a happy person. Recently I met a man who is fifteen years older than me (I am 24) and he is a man I respect very much.

I do not love him, for I find it impossible to love a man in that sense, but I think he is very worthwhile. We talk together as though we have known each other all our lives. We both enjoy movies and swimming and reading books. When he kisses me, however, I feel as though I cannot stand it. I just want to be free of his embrace, if you know what I mean. That is the only thing wrong. In every other way, we are perfect.

He does not know anything about me, or my Lesbianism. Now he wants to marry me. I would like to marry him too. I would like to have children and live a normal life so bad! Yet I am afraid to marry him because of the way I feel when he wants to be close to me. Sometimes I have to restrain myself from hitting him when he puts his arms around me. I feel like scratching his face. I know this is terrible, but it is the way I feel.

What I am writing to you about is, do you think if we got married this would change? He is a good person, Miss Aldrich, and I do not want to hurt him. If you were me what would you do?

Anything you can say to advise me on this matter I would be very grateful to hear.

Thank you for listening to all this and for anything you might advise.

Sincerely yours,
Miss G.J.

Last, a letter from Ohio:

Dear Ann Aldrich,

I am at the point of suicide. I honestly mean that. I have thought of slashing my wrists or jumping out of a window. I am one of those transvestites you write about. If you were to see me on the street, you would think I was a man. I live with my sister, who is an invalid, and I support us. Where I live they know what I am and I am a town joke. My sister taunts me and calls me a lady-lover, but I swear to you I have not once even kissed a woman. In this place if I did that they would tar and feather me.

I am so lost for what to do. I work at . . . . a factory, and there the girls hardly speak to me. One of the men is nice but he is the only one.

You see I really do not look like a woman at all. I have hair on my arms and face and legs like a man, and I am big. If I let my hair grow and wore dresses I would just look like something from a circus, as if I didn't now.

I can't get out of this town because my sister needs me. I would be afraid anyway in a strange city. But my life is a hell. I just want one day of not being a freak, one day when someone will talk to me, or smile at me (instead of laugh at me) or ask me to their place to see them. I just want one day of being like other people. I have always been the way I am, and there is no reason to expect better. Sometimes I wonder why nobody stopped me from dressing like I did. That might have made a difference when I was little. But I grew up in the depression when my folks were poor and just as glad to have me wear my overalls and work shirts. I guess I would have made a funny girl anyway.

No, I don't want your sympathy. I don't know exactly what I do want, but I found a copy of your book in the drug store, and it was the first time I read anything that said there were people like me. Yes, I read THE WELL OF LONELINESS, but the woman in that was rich and attractive and had a family who cared about her. That would make a difference.

I suppose I just want to say thanks for writing that book. It doesn't help me, but maybe it'll keep some kid from being like me if she reads it in time, or her folks do.

Best wishes,
M.L.

16.   A FINAL WORD

In the small New England boarding school where I spent my teens, the halls along the various dormitories were traditionally named after one or the other of Charles Dickens' novels. I lived in David Copperfield. On the hall above me there lived two girls who were considered by all of us to be incredibly distasteful. We called them "Birdlegs" and "Wheezy."

All of us in this boarding school enjoyed crushes on one another; many of us wrote passionate love notes to our crushes; and a few of us, after light bell, risked expulsion by braving the dark corridors that led to the other's room—if the other had a single, or an understanding roommate who was willing to trade beds for the night. Many times embraces were undertaken under the guise of demonstrating how we would like a man to kiss us or hold us; many times they were proffered as giggling, clumsy sessions of playfulness, with no name for them understood, nor any purpose; and sometimes they were the secret, tender-sighing tremulous sort that were clearly realized between two girls, and most carefully concealed from all the others.

But "Birdlegs" and "Wheezy" were in the throes of a *grande passion*. As so often happens fact is much more ironical and seemingly "contrived" than fiction could ever be allowed to be—for the pair roomed together along that hall named after Dickens' novel *Hard Times*.

"Birdlegs" was a rather lovely girl with long blond hair, bright green eyes, and a shy sort of whispery voice. "Wheezy" was short, with an unusually well-developed figure for a fifteen year old, and a pretty, red-cheeked face. Their nicknames were earned not so much for the fact that the former has very thin, stick-like legs, and the latter had asthma—but more for the reason that this pair made everyone nervous, and I suppose without our really understanding it—self-conscious.

In the modern-day jargon, they were really just too much!

Of their room along Hard Times, they made an island. They were always in there with the door shut, and the sign, issued to all of us, posted on the outside: NO AD . . . by our honor we were sworn never to crash a NO AD sign, as was the faculty. The signs were issued with the rather optimistic thought that there were times when a girl wanted an hour of private meditation and prayer. Few of us bothered with the sign save for rare days when contraband in the form of candy or cigarettes could be smuggled in, and devoured with a relative feeling of security. But "Birdlegs" and "Wheezy" always had the sign up. We could hear them laughing and fighting and reading poems aloud, and sometimes we couldn't hear them for a long time, and that was even more annoying.

The reactions of all of us were both shocked and indignant.

We said:

"We ought to report them! It gives all of us a bad name!"

"We don't want them back next year!"

"We ought to get them out right now! What if it gets around that this school is like *that*!"

"Birdlegs" and "Wheezy" had managed to point up to all of us an inner guilt, a fear, a revulsion.

We said:

"A crush is one thing, but they're queer!"

"They're actually serious!"

"They're real Lesbians!"

Together we shed our skin by making up a petition to the faculty to condemn the girls on Hard Times.

There were over 75 signatures when the principal received it, and the following evening, the 75 who had signed it, were called to the principal's salon for a "chat."

With unusually intelligent concern, our headmistress asked us to listen to her before we spoke:

She said:

"I want all of you, for just awhile, to imagine something. Imagine a world—exactly like our own, save for one thing. In this world there is a different mores from ours. In this world men love men; women love women. You, each one of you, are the same person you are at this minute. As young women, you are attracted to young men. You always have been. But it is wrong. You know it is wrong.

"All right, you are misfits, mavericks—queers. Imagine this. You are out of step with everything and everyone around you. What are you going to do? Can you change? You know it is wrong? Is that knowledge sufficient to make you change, or does it happen that despite that knowledge, despite censure and sin, you find yourself looking at a young man and thinking him attractive?

"What is your answer? You are afraid to ask anyone, for fear they will call you names, despise you, make up a petition against you . . . Suppose the young man you think attractive returns your affection? Can you simply reject him? Imagine that.

"Imagine that world and you in it. You are wrong. You did not intend to be wrong. You don't know how it happened that you became as you are. You only know you are not like the others.

"Imagine that, and then tell me, in this world wouldn't you welcome kindliness? Wouldn't you deserve some remote sympathy until you were able to be helped in some way? Wouldn't you think it a godless hell if those around you, instead of thanking God for their health and normality, turned on you for your lack of it?

"Sit and imagine this for one minute, and then we will open the discussion about your petition."

Our petition was destroyed by unanimous agreement. Whatever steps were taken after that by our headmistress, we never knew, but "Birdlegs" and "Wheezy" did not return to school the following year.

Perhaps at that age, and in that situation, we were more easily able to imagine that world our headmistress described. Perhaps like myself, a few others find it even more easy to imagine today. In theory, it is a simple thing to ask of another, to put yourself in somebody else's place. But in practice, the prejudices of the average human being snowball once such an idea is presented.

We say: "But would you want your sister to marry one?" when someone says: "Try to put yourself in the Negro's place."

We say: "But they'll corrupt our children" when someone says: "Try to understand the homosexual and tolerate him in society."

The truth is that probably few white men's sisters would want to marry a Negro, just as few Negroes would want to marry them; and in any case, there could be a far worse mistake for both, than the supposed mistake of intermarriage. The truth is, that our children who are "corrupted" are not corrupted by a homosexual per se, but by psychotics, heterosexuals or homosexuals—both groups have their share.

Homosexuality is a way of life few people have chosen. They have denied it, fought it, suffered it, and accepted it, but rarely have they chosen it.

At the end of A. T. Fitzroy's *Despised and Rejected* (1918), the female character complains:

"Everybody seems to think you're abnormal because you like to be . . . As if being different from other people weren't curse enough in itself!"

The lesbian as you have seen her in these pages has rarely been that "gay" girl she labels herself. Like normal people she makes an attempt to be a part of some faction of society, but her antics and her capers, her high points and her low points, her attempts to appear like everyone else, are slightly grotesque and pathetic when viewed alongside similar situations among heterosexual folk. She is still a freak, and what renders her a freak, is the fact that no matter her little worlds, in the larger world she is out of step.

Ford and Beach in a recent anthropological study found that in 49 out of 76 of the primitive societies they studied, some form of homosexual activity was considered normal and acceptable. For example, a North African tribe, expected all men and boys to engage in homosexual sodomy, and they thought a man peculiar if he did not have both male and female affairs. The Kerakis of New Guinea saw to it that their young men were introduced to anal intercourse at puberty by the older men, and their bachelorhood was spent doing the same to other initiates. Time after time among primitive literature, historical literature, and scientific literature we have found ample evidence that there existed worlds where homosexuality was not only normal, but often very natural and indigenous to its peoples.

However that may be, despite any explanations, rationalizations, or justifications for homosexual behavior, the cliche: *no man is an island* holds. Childhood is a kingdom where no one cares about being different, but when the world is grown up and the individual grown up with it, the homosexual lives on an island in our society. Surely he cannot help but be lonely for the mainland of Real People, and nostalgic for the time when he didn't care about being different and was thus a part of that mainland. Some homosexuals try to recapture that kingdom by pretending they still don't care. The majority do care, but don't know what to do about it.

In a sense there will always be lesbians who live on Hard Times with a No Ad sign on their doors. There will be those who want to sign petitions against these lesbians, and those more kindly disposed, who want to reason with the petition-signers. Sometimes there will be lesbians *among* the petition-signers; those who know they are, and those who don't.

Out of it all there is no answer—but only questions. Psychologists, theologians, sociologists, psychiatrists, anthropologists, writers, parents, and the lesbian herself, may one day see a seminar realized, which will probe this well of loneliness, and provide some of the answers.

THE END

AFTERWORD
PRODUCTIVE CONTRADICTIONS

Every Lesbian who reads this book will be angered,
pleased, and stimulated. What more can [a] book offer?
— B.G., "Ann Aldrich Does a Retake"

We, Too, Must Love (1958) was the second of five books Marijane Meaker wrote under the name Ann Aldrich. By the time she published it, Aldrich had already achieved a national reputation among lesbian readers and writers. Few of her readers were neutral about her; she was lauded or reviled, but she was not ignored. This makes it all the more puzzling that her contributions to lesbian culture and history have not been more acknowledged; at the very least it is significant that Aldrich achieved national celebrity in the gay world of the 1950s.

Conventional histories of the 1950s tend to see that decade as repressed and buttoned down, and most standard literary histories of gay and lesbian writing tacitly agree with that assumption, passing over that decade in relative silence. Very recently, scholars have begun to focus attention on writers and activists who dissented from Cold War ideology and who critiqued the naturalness of the heteronormative nuclear family, but their insights have not quite reached the now-entrenched story of how gay writing developed in the twentieth century.[1]

The canonical list of twentieth-century lesbian writers, for example, tends to focus on the modernists, paying special attention to Paris. That list includes figures like Gertrude Stein, Natalie Barney, Djuna Barnes, and for a few lugubrious chapters, Radclyffe Hall, and then the list leaps into the sixties and seventies, when lesbian and feminist publishing produced a wealth of literature ranging from novels to plays to poetry to political manifestos. If 1950s writers appear in bibliographies, they are usually represented by Ann Bannon, who wrote the much reprinted Beebo Brinker series of lesbian pulps for Gold Medal Press, or by Vin Packer, whose claim to fame is that she wrote *Spring Fire* (1952), the first lesbian pulp written by a United States writer. Ironically, although Marijane Meaker was the writer behind both Vin Packer and Ann Aldrich (she was Ann Bannon's mentor as well), Aldrich has been all but forgotten, obscured by the handful of pulp writers—Bannon, Valerie Taylor, and ironically, Vin Packer—whose novels have come to represent both the genre and the era. When Aldrich appears in contemporary accounts, her achievements are accompanied by the criticism of those contemporaries who dismissed her as a benighted writer who suffered from an internalized homophobia that tainted her journalistic reports on lesbianism.

Many of her first readers would have been surprised by such an assessment. For them, Aldrich illuminated their understanding of the gay world, initiating debate rather than closing it down. Her books emphasized the sophistication, sociability, complicated friendship networks and customs, elaborate romantic strategies, and even the lively sexual intrigues of various lesbian cultures in New York. Indeed, revisiting the New York of Aldrich's *We, Too, Must Love* with the advantage of hindsight makes clear that Aldrich is a key link between early twentieth-century lesbian writers and the impassioned and political lesbians writing after Stonewall, between the earnest politics of the early homophile movement and the deceptively playful politics of the queer movement. Provocative and discerning, committed to representing the diversity that characterized and sometimes divided lesbian life in New York, Ann Aldrich's work explodes views of the 1950s as timid, apolitical, or sexually phobic. Aldrich also shatters the consensus that pre–Stonewall gay politics must have been tentative, assimilationist, or strategically ameliorative. In that sense, Aldrich queers our idea of what it meant to live as a lesbian in the fifties. She also queers the idea of what it meant to speak as a lesbian. One of the main attractions of her work was that she was frank about her own lesbianism, arguing that it gave her an authority that transcended the entrenched expertise of medical and psychiatric professionals who claimed authority about sexual "deviants."

We, Too, Must Love is a fascinating document because it seems so historically anomalous, but it is also a great read. Aldrich weaves together stories about the intersecting lives of extraordinarily different lesbian couples—each of whom holds different definitions of what it means to be a lesbian and to live a fulfilling life with another woman. All of this is framed by an unparalleled contemporary social history of New York in the fifties. *We, Too, Must Love* is groundbreaking precisely because it is not an exposé of frightened, closeted women tortured by their difference from "normal" people. Tortured women appear, to be sure, but with few exceptions they are tortured not by the fear that their deviance will be discovered by their mothers, but by the fear that their manifold charms will go undiscovered by the gorgeous woman across the bar. *We, Too, Must Love*'s lesbians are less concerned with figuring out the big questions about gay identity than in figuring out "all the little ways of being gay," as Gertrude Stein once phrased it (1999, 22). Aldrich's journalism is attuned to the significance of everyday details, experiences, and struggles within lesbian culture. If *We, Too, Must Love* deserves a special place in lesbian and gay cultural and literary history because it took the pulse of the interlocked quotidian lives of the inhabitants of New York's lesbian cultures, it is also important because it raised the blood pressure of other lesbian writers and thus acted as a kind of counterstatement to more generally-known official descriptions of what it meant to live as a "normal" lesbian in the fifties.

In this Afterword, I will discuss the extraordinary circumstances of Aldrich's career—the conditions that allowed her to write as a lesbian about lesbian life—as well as the response that her work elicited in the late fifties and early sixties from the Daughters of Bilitis (DOB), the only national organization of lesbians then working to secure greater visibility and acceptance for all homosexuals. Some of the DOB's objections to Aldrich were grounded in its members' belief that Aldrich had shown too many internal conflicts in the lesbian community; that she had therefore confirmed the general belief that lesbians were unhappy and neurotic. Yet the DOB's concerted attempts first to cultivate her and then to discredit her ultimately produced one of Aldrich's most valuable historical lessons, in some sense also the real subject of the text itself: Lesbians have never been a homogeneous group. They have argued over what it meant to be a lesbian and to belong to a lesbian culture from the moment a lesbian culture can be imagined to have existed. *We, Too, Must Love* describes lesbians of different social classes, educational levels, and professional aspirations; and the volume reveals how different lesbian groups made their own smaller communities, how they interpreted gender identity, political commitments, the possibility of meaningful relationships with men, of making a family, and even how they turned different sexual desires into practices. (The text is largely silent on the matter of racial differences, which itself tells us a good deal about what counted as a meaningful difference in the lesbian communities of the fifties, although in the final chapter Aldrich does use interracial marriage as an analogy for same sex love).[2] Aldrich understood that such differences have always been constitutive of the fantastical and idealized "lesbian community," and that ignoring those differences in the name of a progressive orthodoxy or a unified public image closed down other paths to historical and social change.

Ann Aldrich's Work

In 1955 Ann Aldrich inaugurated what would become a five book series with *We Walk Alone*, which she followed with *We, Too, Must Love* (1958), *Carol in a Thousand Cities* (1960) *We Two Won't Last* (1963), and finally *Take a Lesbian to Lunch* (1972). All but the last book were published by Gold Medal, the division of Fawcett Publishing specializing in reasonably-priced paperback originals. By the time she was writing *We, Too, Must Love* Aldrich undoubtedly did not think of herself as a "pulp" writer, but as the inheritor of a specifically lesbian literary tradition, as well as a writer in dialogue with mainstream discussions of sexuality. Its title, for example, echoes Gale Wilhelm's famous novel *We Too Are Drifting* (1935), and the text itself is filled with self-reflexive citations of other works, prominently Radclyffe Hall's *The Well of Loneliness* (1928) and in one tongue and cheek instance, an elaborately casual reference to Vin Packer. Just after she released *We, Too, Must Love*, Aldrich edited *Carol in a Thousand Cities*, an important collection of writing about women's sexuality that reinforced her centrality in debates that were increasingly traversing gay and straight publications alike, an occurrence in no small part due to her own work.[3]

In her first book, *We Walk Alone*, Aldrich established her credentials. That book is in large part a collection of facts ranging from an explanation of the historical world of Sappho and a reading of her poetry to a list of the sodomy laws in every state in the union. Although her voice is often wonderfully biting, it is more temperate than her later work. In this first volume, Aldrich presents the views of authorities—from medicine, law, and psychiatry—often summarizing their arguments in order to respond to and sometimes contradict their theories point by point. For much of the book, that is, she concentrates on a question that seemed to underwrite every public or "expert" discussion of homosexuality: What makes a lesbian a lesbian? Was she born that way, or did she become a lesbian through choice, or because of a traumatic childhood event? Could she be cured? What could be done? Viewing these popular theories seriously allowed Ann Aldrich to establish herself as an expert in two worlds, which, she argued, had not sufficiently engaged one another. She spoke as a lesbian, drawing on her first-hand knowledge of New York life, and she spoke as a researcher, able to find, discuss, evaluate, and assess medical and cultural stereotypes about lesbians. That particular combination of viewpoints gives *We Walk Alone* its sometimes jarring mix of, on the one hand, faith in a psychiatric model that casts lesbians as abnormal and sick and, on the other hand, a shrewd recognition of structurally produced gender inequalities that predicates a more modern social constructionist reading.

For many readers, *We Walk Alone* pulled back a veil, revealing a vibrant world that had up until that point been discussed in major public venues mainly by medical and legal experts, who spoke from a vantage point outside of and above their subjects. Such professional observers might have been interested in the psychological or familial dynamics of homosexuality, and they might even in some cases have been sympathetic, calling for "tolerance" of the sexual deviant. But very rarely were they interested in the social dynamics of how real lesbians formed relationships and found jobs, how they communicated with their families and where they met friends, where they vacationed, and how they remembered their pasts—how, in other words, they lived day to day lives that were both ordinary and extraordinary, lives that were not always organized around fitting into dominant heterosexual culture. Especially for lesbian readers, the glimpses Ann Aldrich's first book gave of that ordinary, everyday homosexual world were maddening or heartening. Some found her work inaccurate, as pathologizing and judgmental as that of the psychiatric establishment, but many more found her work tantalizing and revelatory, a map of an urban world where lesbians did not need to live in utter secrecy.

We Walk Alone sold like hotcakes—Marijane Meaker has reported that each of her Gold Medal books had a print run of 400,000—and the first book went through multiple editions, becoming one of Gold Medal's bestselling titles for 1955. More than the number of books flying off the drugstore and train station racks, the book's significance for gay readers in particular is confirmed by the fact that it was promptly reviewed in the handful of major gay and lesbian periodicals in existence at the time. One such magazine, *The Ladder*, the official publication of the DOB, began one of its earliest issues with the proceedings of a public forum in which members discussed the impact and potential value of Aldrich's work. But the organized, or official, gay responses to the book are just the tip of the iceberg. Perhaps the best measure of how well Aldrich had identified the need for a serious, even erudite, book about lesbians by a lesbian lies in the overwhelming number of individuals who took the time to write to her. *We Walk Alone* inspired hundreds of readers, both gay and straight, to send letters describing how her work had affected them. The letters included pleas for more information, confessions about the writers themselves, and questions about various family members who had fallen under suspicion of abnormality. Some were angry, some were relieved, some were confused, but they were all in some way moved enough to want to correspond with her.

The book's sales prompted Gold Medal to pressure Aldrich to write a follow-up, but in some sense, the sheer volume of letters Aldrich received should also be seen as an important indicator of the shape the sequel eventually took. *We, Too, Must Love* is less concerned with outsiders' views of lesbians than it is with describing of the inner lives of lesbian couples, less interested in how lesbians transgress the norms of the straight world than in providing a careful account of the internal rules and customs of various lesbian subcultures.

In the 1958 Foreword to *We, Too, Must Love*, for example, Aldrich is not interested in responding to the "official" homophile reactions to the book, nor does she pay much attention to the medical, legal, or psychiatric communities' opinions about homosexuality. One might claim, therefore, that the second volume is not really a sequel to the first, for it does not continue its strategies. Rather, *We, Too, Must Love* is interested in answering what appear to be an overwhelming series of practical, everyday sorts of questions from the readers who had written. Aldrich notes in her 1958 Foreword: "In 1955 I wrote a book called *We Walk Alone*, a study of a lesbian by a lesbian. After its publication, I received hundreds of letters . . . This book is an answer to those letters as well as a supplement to *We Walk Alone*. In it I have written of the whys and wherefores of lesbian life in New York City—as I have known it." She quotes one of the letters she received, in which a reader wistfully writes: "I'm glad you explained to people that we're not all tough, trouser-wearing, cropped-haired aggressive women who hate men and flaunt our ways. . . . I wish there were more to *We Walk Alone*!" The letters told Aldrich that her book had reached readers she had perhaps not even imagined were out there, de facto conferring on her the very expertise she had tried to seize by writing the first book. And yet, readers were also asking her to share a different kind of expertise with them, one that appeared to be more personal, and which although—or perhaps because—it seemed also pedestrian, was rare in publications at that particular moment. It was the sort of expertise—where to find other gay people, what bars and restaurants in New York were hospitable—that had up until that point been circulated mainly by word of mouth, by those in the know. It appeared to some readers to be a specialized form of unwritten information, the circulation of which could both ratify and reveal the workings of gay identity.

Publishing on Sexuality

That's not to say that sexuality, especially homosexuality, was not a major topic for novelists and journalists alike. It was. Aldrich's ability to publish her books, to have them marketed and transported across the country where they would reach different audiences, even her ability to discuss different definitions of lesbianism, was indebted to a publishing industry that recognized and fed public fascination with the twinned topics of psychoanalysis and sexuality. Motivated by the extraordinary popularity of Kinsey's *Sexual Behavior in the Human Female* (1953) and his cowritten *Sexual Behavior in the Human Male* (1948), publishers did a brisk business in nonfiction work dealing with sexuality, including popular accounts of psychoanalysis and book-length analyses of homosexuality, most of which were written by experts and pitched to a general audience. The mainstream popular media, too, had become intensely interested in the "problem" of homosexuality. *Time* magazine, *The Nation*, and the *New York Times*, for example, all carried stories about "the" homosexual presence, as they tended to call it, in society, concentrating especially on legal reports, such as Great Britain's 1957 Wolfenden Report and on the psychiatric community's assessments of homosexuality's causes and potential cures.[4]

Ann Aldrich's books were not reviewed in mainstream venues like *Time*, but their popularity—indeed, the very fact that they could be published at all—was enabled by the fact that debates about homosexuality had moved from professional communities and journals into more mainstream publications. Aldrich was something of an autodidact in the regnant psychiatric theories of homosexuality; her reportorial accounts of lesbian New York had much more in common with the narrative strategies of mainstream articles and books about homosexuality (including Donald Webster Cory's widely-reviewed 1951 *The Homosexual in America*, which had inspired the first lines of her first book) than they did with the often lurid novels about sexuality in which her publisher, for example, specialized. Even so, the impact of presses like Gold Medal cannot be underestimated in understanding Aldrich's career. The paperback revolution of which Gold Medal was a part took advantage of a generalized public discussion of sexuality, and by publishing writers like Aldrich, paperback houses inevitably changed the very terms of that discussion.

Gold Medal, the publisher of the first four of Aldrich's books, was the division of Fawcett specializing in what we now think of as pulps, more accurately called paperback originals in the case of Gold Medal. Unlike many other paperback lines, Gold Medal did not reprint successful hardback books in soft cover. Gold Medal, by publishing original works in paper, introduced a new set of writers to a new market. Part of the genius of how paperbacking changed readers' patterns of consumption lay in its method of distribution; paperbacks were not only sold in bookstores but more significantly in train stations and drug stores, where they could be purchased by commuters or casual shoppers drawn to their often lurid covers and mildly titillating blurbs and back cover copy. For gay readers, the ability to pick up a "gay" book from a rack of other similar books in a fairly anonymous place was safer and easier than trying some of the mail-order houses, or, if they were lucky enough to have access to one, a bookstore with specialized books.

Paperbacks were deliberately inexpensive, using cheaply-made paper (thus the name "pulp"), and they were small enough to fit into a coat pocket. Although many such paperbacks, including the Gold Medal edition of *We, Too, Must Love*, had sensational packaging, a great many of them contained well-crafted and subtle texts. Although there is no necessary correlation between the historical or aesthetic innovation of a text and its packaging, cheaply-made pulps often published stories that would not have been considered by conventional houses, a factor that was of especial importance for gay and lesbian writers and readers. For this reason, a great deal of scholarship on pulps and pulp presses in lesbian literary and cultural histories has focused on how fiction pushed against entrenched cultural and sexual proprieties (Meeker 2005; Stryker 2001; Zimet 1999). Gay and straight scholars alike have examined how the pulps brokered the appearance of social minorities as subjects within and as writers of novels. Scholars have also described the relatively formulaic narrative conventions of pulps, which allowed lesbians to establish themselves as authors and as writers (Foote 2005; Keller 2005; Walters 1989; Villarejo 1999). For lesbian novelists especially, the conventions of paperback publishing demanded an unhappy ending for lesbian fictional couples. Indeed, while paperbacking ensured that Aldrich's work would reach a market (though it certainly didn't anticipate the exact gay market her work produced), it also enforced some meaningful restrictions on it.

In particular, censorship was a serious threat to all publishers, especially those specializing in fiction. In the late fifties and early sixties, obscenity laws were local, varying from state to state and even from town to town. They were often only sporadically enforced, and only slowly being challenged, often by

bookstore owners and paperback publishers on whom censors
tended to come down most severely. Even though providing
scientific information or practicing some form of journalism
was often encouraged by presses as a way to protect themselves
from the morals charges on which censorship laws were based,
publishing houses and their writers pushed hard against restrictions. We can take as an example Gold Medal's production
choices for *We, Too, Must Love*. The book's cover has the requi-
site female body, tastefully turned away from the viewer, and an
approving blurb from psychiatrist Richard H. Hoffman testify-
ing to the book's usefulness. That fine line between scientific
value and sexual titillation does not structure what Aldrich
wrote, but it does define the poles between which publishers
who feared the censors tended to place their books.

Gay Organizing and Publishing in the Fifties

By the time *We, Too, Must Love* appeared many people bought
it because it was an Aldrich book. She had tapped into a specialized lesbian readership by providing what they had not yet
seen: what it meant to be and live as a lesbian. In some ways,
she had introduced readers to a world in which it was possible
to live an ordinary life as a lesbian. In the process, though, she
had also managed affront the Daughters of Bilitis (DOB), the
largest lesbian organization in the country.

The DOB had benefited in much the same way as had
Aldrich from wide-spread interest in homosexuality, as well as
from the development of new ways of talking about what sexuality meant. It was formed in 1955, and in 1956, the first
issue of its magazine *The Ladder* was produced. The DOB
was only one among a number of important gay organizations that maintained a national profile in the fifties. It was
socially and politically active, organizing meetings and discussion groups and alerting members to legal problems on the
horizon. It also regularly supported other gay organizations in

political struggles, urging its members, for example, to keep up with and give their support to the gay men's magazine *ONE* during its legal battle with the post office.[5]

Although Aldrich was aware of the DOB by the time she published *We, Too, Must Love*, and often directed letter writers to their organization, they did not make much of an impression on her work. For one thing, the experience of lesbians on the west coast was very different than that of the New Yorkers in whom Aldrich was most interested. For another, the DOB was still very small, and despite its national ambitions, the day to day life of lesbians was shaped far more by local and regional customs. Nonetheless, Aldrich's work was of immediate interest to that organization, for the DOB was interested in using *The Ladder* to coordinate local and national conversations about gay life and identity. Every issue of *The Ladder* included a four-point statement of purpose designed to facilitate the integration of the homosexual into society. In part, the group hoped to accomplish its aims by educating lesbians as well as straight people about the meaning and origin of homosexuality by sponsoring dialogues between themselves and competent professionals and experts. The DOB also used *The Ladder* to publish opinion pieces and letters from readers about the shape and the direction of gay culture. Favorite topics included how lesbians should dress, how they should comport themselves in public, as well as how they could find or make a community in other parts of the country. The editors of *The Ladder* were keenly aware of exactly how much information was circulating about homosexuality, and they dedicated a great deal of time to book reviewing and textual analysis, taking on publications by members of the psychiatric community as well as fiction that seemed to them either edifying or pernicious. Aldrich, not surprisingly, appeared on their radar very quickly indeed.

Despite the fact that both Aldrich and the DOB were

working at the same time, and were trying to address a public that in some ways had become more sophisticated in its tolerance for discussions of sexuality (if not in its tolerance for homosexuals themselves), the DOB and Ann Aldrich were like oil and water from the first. In one of the earliest numbers of *The Ladder*, the DOB recognized the impact of *We Walk Alone* by carrying an article about a public discussion it had sponsored about Ann Aldrich. A few people had praised her. Del Martin, for instance, had urged a more sophisticated reading of Aldrich than the hostile reading that seemed to be emerging from roundtable participants. She argued that "too many homophile readers were looking for 'affirmation'" and then pointed out that books printed by commercial houses had to follow certain guidelines in representations of gay life in order to be printed at all. (1957, 16). The logic is a little skewed here, giving credit to Aldrich with one hand and taking it away with the other, but what is important is that Del Martin's contribution is one of the few that gave Aldrich any credit at all. Most of the forum's participants registered a querulous dissatisfaction with her work.

The opening paragraph of the review argues: "for all Miss Aldrich's good intentions she did not achieve her purpose and failed to balance her more bizarre examples of Lesbianism with those who have attained adjustment and are useful, productive citizens" (1957, 16). The last paragraph echoes the anemic acceptance of the first: "It was generally agreed that Miss Aldrich 'tried', that hers is a valid contribution to Lesbian literature (of which there is so little) if not taken too seriously or considered 'gospel' by those of limited experience" (1957, 17). At the time Aldrich appeared to ignore completely the DOB's earnest critiques. Her most sustained response to the DOB's criticisms took the form of a devastating essay in *Carol in a Thousand Cities* in which she portrayed the DOB as doctrinaire and intolerant of heterosexuality (something Aldrich herself was accused of in an otherwise positive review in *ONE*). Over the years the DOB and "Miss Aldrich," as they liked to call her in print, exchanged barbs; as late as 1972, in a review of Aldrich's last book *Take a Lesbian To Lunch* (1972), "Gene Damon" (Barbara Grier) refers to Aldrich rather dramatically as "our old nemesis" (Grier 1976, 272) and chastises her in an unusually long review for, among other things, describing *The Ladder* with "the usual expected venom" and complaining that Aldrich had implied that the magazine had not progressed—that it is "about where it was eight to ten years ago" (273).[6]

The occasional volleys in print between Aldrich and the DOB are vivid reminders of Ann Aldrich's cultural importance; indeed, the DOB doubtless contributed to her celebrity by using her as a scapegoat for the arguments and contradictions that she had pointed out as existant in gay and lesbian culture. Historian Martin Meeker, consulting the archive detailing the personal and public exchanges between Aldrich and the DOB, makes the persuasive argument that the repeated contretemps between Aldrich and the DOB were expressions of a larger concern about lesbian self-representation. From the perspective of today's fractious gay and lesbian public sphere, it seems clear that the DOB and Ann Aldrich had more in common than otherwise. Indeed, looking at them together, we can see that the DOB was not as assimilationist as its later critics charged, and it is also clear that Ann Aldrich was nowhere near as conservative as her contemporary critics charged.

In hindsight, it is easier to see that Ann Aldrich and the DOB existed in a productive tension, asking many of the same kinds of questions, although in a different register of debate. For Martin Meeker the central questions posed by the DOB and Aldrich converged around the most politically efficacious strategies for lesbian self-representation. What kinds of communication would be most beneficial for helping gay and lesbian people achieve social recognition and rights? In retrospect, it also seems that many of the problems that Aldrich and the DOB recognized as imminent in a growing lesbian culture look a little antiquated and even a little quaint to contemporary readers, although some seem strangely familiar. Do people choose to be gay? Is gayness produced by childhood trauma? Can psychiatric care remediate gay people? What makes a butch a butch? Do femmes have it easier? Should butches dress like women in order to pass at work? Should all gay people organize to demand rights? What do lesbians have in common with gay men? Should gay people seek rights or assimilation? What did assimilation mean?

It may be true, as Martin Meeker argues, that the DOB cast itself and Aldrich as opposite poles in a dispute about how lesbians should appear to the general public, and it may also be true that they did so for strategic reasons. But it seems likely that the DOB's grounds for dismissing Aldrich's contributions also had the effect of misreading their similarities in the name of insisting on their differences. It is worth noting, then, that their similarities were many. Some seem small, such as the fact that Aldrich and the DOB insisted that no one could tell who was a lesbian just by looking. Some seem more important, such as their shared belief that the medical establishment needed to take account of the fact that lesbians were capable of choosing their own futures, and that they could be happy in those futures. But most striking is that Aldrich and the DOB shared a powerful belief that print itself mattered, that books could reach people, could change minds, could shape communities. This is in part, of course, why the DOB gave over so much space in *The Ladder* to book reviewing. But it also explains why the DOB disliked Aldrich's work: As a lesbian, she had committed a disloyal act by exposing and publicizing internal contradictions, undercutting the ability of lesbians to present a united front to a potentially hostile culture.

Casting Aldrich as a deliberate dissenter from the still-emerging norms of "the" lesbian community had the unfortunate effect of blinding the DOB to Aldrich's profound sensitivity to local issues and communities with which the DOB was not especially concerned. Aldrich organized *We, Too, Must Love* around some of the very questions that the DOB ignored when it criticized Aldrich. What differences did overlapping lesbian subcultures in a single city experience as meaningful? Which could be ignored? What kinds of harm could lesbians cause for one another by withholding recognition or membership in a given network of friends? How could lesbians move between different lesbian cultures? Aldrich's attention to the fragility of belonging—whether to a relationship, or a friendship group, or a neighborhood—gives us an historical archive enriched by her willingness to look at how communities could splinter as well as come together. That dynamic is precisely what gives her work its historical value, for she shows us how many choices about "ways of being gay" existed in the fifties. Indeed, Aldrich's ability to question lesbian politics, to chafe against pat definitions, and to act as a sort of agitator helped her produce, rather than simply describe, a more sophisticated literary and cultural scene than the one she entered.

Inside Lesbian Cultures

We, Too, Must Love challenged Aldrich's critics, reached out to her readers, and recast some of the topics of her first book. It confirmed her position at the center of overlapping debates about what exactly counted as "lesbian writing" and "lesbian culture," even as it argued in part that there could be no unified definition of "lesbian culture." The book is not like the first one, an insider's response to various outsiders' views of lesbian life. Rather, it is an insider's look at exactly what makes different "ways in being gay" work: what anchors lesbians socially; what informs them intellectually; and what sustains them romantically. *We, Too, Must Love* can be roughly divided into three sections. In the first Aldrich introduces different lesbian couples, paying close attention to the dynamics of their friendships and romantic relationships. In the second section she provides a fascinating social geography of lesbian New York, filling in the background against which the couples' lives unfold. She tours bars, summer resorts, restaurants, and introduces a cast of what we might think of as "minor characters" (other than lesbians themselves) who people these worlds. And finally, in the last section, Aldrich redirects her analytic gaze to herself; she shares an odd and oddly revealing personal story about her own experience in boarding school, as well as a small selection of the letters she received after *We Walk Alone* came out.

Conceived and executed as an extended journalistic report, *We, Too, Must Love* gives the effect of immediacy and transparency, two qualities that paradoxically testify to the artfulness of its construction. The effect of transparency—the feeling that we are looking at raw and unmediated representations of lesbian life—is in part a credit to Aldrich's feeling for the details that make up the inner lives of a given group. It is also, though, a credit to her thorough and unobtrusive ability to navigate different neighborhoods as well as to her observation of certain unspoken rules about how one behaves with other lesbians in public places. The easy balance achieved by her narrative voice, which is simultaneously analytic and participatory, within and outside of the worlds she describes, is perhaps the aspect of the text that provides its bite and poignancy, for Aldrich's ability to represent serious emotions and to analyze their sources lets the text's tone turn on a dime. It can be wearily dismissive of the emotional drama of lesbian life and in the next moment, it will linger over moments of real tenderness between lesbian couples.

If her skill at constructing her narrative persona (a skill we might credit to Meaker's successful career as a novelist, especially her mastery of narrative suspense in the books she wrote as Vin Packer) gives the text its emotional depth, her skill as a journalist gives it forward motion. She has a wonderful ability to pull back from details important for the reader's understanding of the hidden, inner life of a couple to describe how that couple makes daily choices about whom to see and where to go and what to wear. These, of course, tend to be choices about how a couple should socialize, and hence, Aldrich tends to focus the drama of the text on various meetings among different lesbian subcultures. In these carefully orchestrated instances, when couples cross social and geographic boundaries, and when borders between different lesbian subcultures become momentarily permeable, Aldrich slows the text down, describing the participants' conversations, their mute glances at one another, their sudden consciousness of some significant moment. In these instances, Aldrich shows us scenes in which different lesbians, whose inner lives we now know, can come face-to-face with a different version of themselves. That is, she is not only interested in the inner lives of members of lesbian subcultures, she is interested in how they see themselves and one another. (Aldrich's lesbians are largely indifferent to what straight people think of them—most of the straight characters in the text are fools—or they are quite cynical about how to manipulate the perceptions of a straight audience). Ultimately, the complicated pieces of Aldrich's narrative journalism convey a portrait in which, for better or worse, gay cultures establish norms and create narratives about themselves and each other that are both nourishing and destructive. Her insight into that dynamic is both a key to the text itself, as well as one of its great historical contributions.

A positive way to say this is that Aldrich is drawn to a certain kind of friction, a specific sexual and social tension. For her, that tension lies—strangely, given the regnant psychiatric definitions of homosexuality—not in sameness, but in difference, in moments of dissent from the rules, or in moments when norms seem to be suspended. There is no doubt that the text is remarkably frank about the sexual intrigues of lesbians, about the sudden flaring of desire between them. But perhaps the negative way to say this is equally accurate—Aldrich is impatient with how quickly each subculture claims to embody the truth of what it is to be a lesbian, and she is therefore interested in moments when such definitions are challenged. The duality of the text is apparent even in what we might call the narrative arc of each couple. On the one hand, Aldrich's lesbians fall in love and are seduced, they go on vacation and give one another jewelry. They exchange smoldering looks and cry over keepsakes and trinkets. They can kindle and maintain exciting relationships. On the other hand, Aldrich's lesbians seem doomed to a life of repetition. All of the relationships fail, all of the women search endlessly for the loves of their life. They end up knowing everyone's ex, but even the profound jealousy inspired by an ex and all she represents can't really be sustained. The content of their gossip is always the same; the events never change, only the names. They cannot seem to grow. They are prone to alcoholism, loneliness, and they spend their spare time searching for the perfect partner, even if they are already in a relationship. Most depressing in this reading is that for Aldrich, the emotional and social dysfunction her couples experience cannot be charged entirely to the account of a hostile society that forces them to live, misunderstood and forsaken, in the shadows. There is also the responsibility of hostile lesbian societies whose members seem to know at once too much and too little about each another.

Thus, the tension in *We, Too, Must Love* comes from Aldrich's mixture of intense suspicion of and genuine interest in what it means for a lesbian to become part of a group of other lesbians. Using sufficient detail to render the qualities of

life for three different lesbian subcultures, Aldrich then places
their members into conflict. The uptown lesbians have a lot of
money, powerful jobs, and good educations. They attend art
openings, and throw lavish parties. When they go out, they go
to very good restaurants, but unless they are slumming, they
do not go to the dyke bars in the Village. They dress well, in
tasteful and expensive clothes, but they dress, in the main, like
ladies; they do not indicate, except to those in the know, that
they are lesbians. When they wish to talk about their lesbianism, they can do so very fluently in a Freudian idiom, for they
have access to money for analysis. There is usually some
inequality between the partners in a relationship; one has
more money, or is another's boss.

A second group is quasi-intellectual, well-educated,
bohemian, Village lesbians. They are characterized by their
androgyny—they fit neither the dominant cultural stereotype
of normative straight masculinity or femininity. They don't
have much money, but they have ideals. They have small
apartments with shelves of lesbian books, and sometimes they
go to a little neighborhood place for dinner and a drink.
Unashamedly and self-consciously out as lesbians, the Village
bohemians are perceived as faintly silly by the dyke-femme
couples, and as rather militant by the uptown lesbians. They
can't usually afford analysis, but they have the intellectual
vocabulary to discuss lesbian history and literature, which,
because it models different forms of homosexuality for them,
seems to stand them in the place of analysis.

And finally, there is what Aldrich calls the "dyke-femme"
couple, better known to us as a butch-femme couple. That
couple lives in the Village and drinks in dives. The dyke can
rarely keep a job, often because she is perceived to be a man
and then exposed, or because her low educational level pre-
vents her from getting work in the first place. She is economically dependent on her femme, but in Aldrich's report, the

femme wouldn't have it any other way. Economically and socially marginal, the dyke-femme couples are most at risk of being destroyed by an intolerant culture. They are also, according to Aldrich, the most likely to try to claim public space by going regularly to their local bar. If the dyke-femme couple wants to discuss what it means to be a lesbian or to live a lesbian life, they need not resort to literature or psychoanalysis (although one of the femmes in the text is in what Aldrich considers very poorly administered analysis). They are, perhaps more than the other women in Aldrich's text, sure of who they are, and sure of what kind of lesbians they are in the ordinary everyday way of being gay.

But it is exactly such a conviction that gives the narrative of *We, Too, Must Love* its edgy combination of sympathy and judgment. Let's take the butch-femme couple—Miki, the femme, and Morgan, the dyke—as our example of how Aldrich tries to show how the combination of their confident self-knowledge with their casual judgments of how other lesbians choose to live as lesbians (and the corresponding judgments of other lesbians about them) is at once empowering and limiting. The dyke-femme couple is a good example because its members' differences from the other groups are so obvious, manifest in their class position, their leisure pursuits, their choice about how to inhabit their gender, their public visibility. They are, as well, most easily judged by other kinds of lesbians. Aldrich writes, "The scorn with which the average Lesbian views her transvestite [butch] sister is manifold," and includes a sampling of the stereotypes lesbians have about butch-femme couples. "They're *really* sick. I don't even think of them as homosexuals," says one (39). They "ruin gay bars. They bring in the bad element, the cheap chorus-girl type, and they attract attention to the bar by their dress," says another (40). The stereotypes are all-too familiar, congregating around the butch's visibility, the femme's hyperfeminized sexuality, and the class distinctions that structure how lesbians inhabit and therefore judge the proper performance of gender and sexuality.[7] Aldrich seems neutral about these statements, but she includes a critique of the common psychiatric idiom about dyke femme relationships's immaturity, calling it "glib," following it with the remark that the "femme who is attracted to the transvestite often is simply a carbon copy of the kind of woman she would be if she were a heterosexual" (31). It's a classic Aldrich statement—on its face perverse and judgmental, and yet strangely liberating because it is based not on proscriptive lesbian community norms but on a consideration of structurally and psychically produced gender categories.

Even as Aldrich describes how the most common judgments about Miki and Morgan misread the complexity of their relationship and the conscious and deliberate way that they choose to be together in public and in private, she reveals that their definition of how to live an ordinary, meaningful lesbian life is just as exclusive. She closes their section of the narrative by reporting an unnamed femme's contempt for the Village lesbian clique: "They all look alike. You can't tell the dyke from the lady; they're like two peas in a pod. They're queer queers if you ask me," (47–8). Aldrich's constant repetitions of the judgments lesbians pass about one another makes the text a little bit depressing—none of the women seems happy for very long, and many seem to feel enormous pressure to conform to the norms of her group—but it also gives the text the material with which to build an irrefutable argument against any stable or unified definition of "the lesbian" or "the lesbian community."

This is not to say that Aldrich's persona in the text is above making judgments about how people defined and understood lesbianism. She most certainly is not. Readers will doubtless notice that *We, Too, Must Love* both jabs at and embraces psychoanalysis, and that Aldrich tends to use the word "abnormal"

rather more often than is comfortable in a text in which ortho-
doxies about identities and lifestyles are in question. But she is
also quite blunt when she argues that lesbians are not "freaks"
because they are not "normal," and is refreshingly common-
sensical in her belief that the source of most lesbians' suffering
is not from "the need to have society accept her as one with the
heterosexual. It is usually the need for the Lesbian to accept
herself" (11). And she is also unafraid to turn her gaze upon
herself; her final chapter recounts a story of how she was
involved in a thwarted witch hunt against two lesbians in
boarding school. She does not spare herself, and she does not
make excuses for her youthful behavior; rather she lets the
episode stand as the most trenchant example of one of her
major points: there is simply no mechanical correlation
between who we seem to be and who we are, and there is no
way to predict who we will become from who we are now.

We, Too, Must Love is a product of its era; it is not ahead of
its time. But that is exactly what makes it so interesting for us
now. Because it is so truly of its moment, clearly marked by
some of its prejudices and assumptions, *We, Too, Must Love*
shows us that moment as ripe with possibilities for emerging
lesbian communities. Aldrich was of her moment in her very
capacity for contradiction. The late fifties were not dominated
by a single orthodoxy, a single theory, a single way of being
gay. Aldrich's text, focused intently on the conflicts that drive
the inner lives of three lesbian communities, is skeptical of any
unified theory of lesbian behavior, origins, and desires. And
because she insists on the importance of the local—New York
and its neighborhoods—in the formation of different sexual
cultures, she reminds readers that gay and lesbian history did
not develop in the same way everywhere in the country.
Despite the universalizing gestures of medical authorities, lesbians and gay men experienced and lived their sexuality
against and within particular places. Aldrich's politics can be

contradictory, and her descriptions of lesbian life can be piti-
less. Taken point by point, the text can be frustrating. But
taken as a whole, it is a marvel. Aldrich's sensitivity towards the
harm that norms inflict on individuals, and her recognition
that the norms of a minority culture could be just as harmful
as the norms of a hegemonic culture make her contradictory
streak productive as we perpetually work to discover future
ways of being gay—and to rediscover their multiple histories—we have not yet been able to see.

Stephanie Foote
Urbana, Illinois
June 2006

Notes

1. See *WSQ: Gender and Culture in the 1950s*.

2. Meaker's memoir, Highsmith makes it clear that Meaker was socially
progressive. In fact, Patricia Highsmith's ethnic prejudices finally confirmed
to Meaker that they had very little in common.

3. Aldrich titled *Carol in a Thousand Cities* (1960) after the famous final
words of Clare Morgan's important novel *The Price of Salt* (1952), in which
the two central female characters do not come to the tragic end usual at that
time for lesbian fiction. Clare Morgan was the pseudonym of Patricia Highsmith, with whom Marijane Meaker was romantically involved in the late
fifties and early sixties.

4. For more on discussions of sexuality in different media, see my Afterword to the Feminist Press 2006 reprint of Aldrich's *We Walk Alone*.

5. *ONE*, which was directed mainly at men (but which ran the only
review of Aldrich's work that recognized her tendency to satirize), began
publishing in 1953, and in 1955 the Mattachine Society began the monthly
Mattachine Review.

6. In his excellent essay "A Queer and Contested Medium" Martin
Meeker details the entire history of exchanges between the DOB and Ann
Aldrich, which included numerous letters to the editors about the destruc-
tiveness of Aldrich's work as well as personal correspondence from the editors after *We, Too, Must Love* was released inviting Marijane Meaker to meet
them in New York, an invitation she seems to have declined (2005).

7. Aldrich's work on dyke-femme couples makes it an excellent addition to literature about butch-femme lesbians. It resonates with Joan Nestle's collection *The Persistent Desire* (1992) as well as with Madeline Davis and Elizabeth Kennedy's *Boots of Leather, Slippers of Gold* (1993).

Works Cited

A.C.R.1958. "Review of *We, Too, Must Love.*" *ONE* 6:5:29.

Aldrich, Ann. 1955. *We Walk Alone*. Greenwich, CT: Fawcett/Gold Medal.

———. 1958. *We, Too, Must Love*. Greenwich, CT: Fawcett/Gold Medal.

———, ed. 1960. *Carol in a Thousand Cities*. Greenwich, CT: Fawcett/Gold Medal.

———. 1963. *We Two Won't Last*. Greenwich, CT: Fawcett/Gold Medal.

———. 1972. *Take a Lesbian to Lunch*. New York: McFadden.

———. 2006. *We Walk Alone*. [1950]. New York: The Feminist Press at CUNY.

"Aldrich 'Walks Alone.'" 1957. *The Ladder* 1:9 (June): 16–17.

B.G. 1958. "Ann Aldrich Does a Retake." *The Ladder* (January):12.

Cory, Donald Webster. 1957. *The Homosexual in America: A Subjective Approach*. [1951]. New York: Greenberg Publishers.

Davis, Madeline and Elizabeth Kennedy. 1993. *Boots of Leather, Slippers of Gold*. New York: Routledge.

Foote, Stephanie. 2005. "Deviant Classics: Pulps and the Making of Lesbian Print Culture." *Signs* 31:1 (Autumn):169–189.

Grier, Barbara. 1976. *Lesbiana: Book Reviews from The Ladder 1966–1972*. Tallahassee, FL: Naiad Press.

Hall, Radclyffe. 1928. *The Well of Loneliness*. New York: Anchor Books.

Keller, Yvonne. 2005. "'Was it Right to Love Her Brother's Wife So Passionately?' Lesbian Pulp Novels and US Lesbian Identity, 1950-1965." *American Quarterly* 57:1 (June): 385–410.

Kinsey, Alfred C. 1953. *Sexual Behavior in the Human Female*. Philadelphia: Saunders.

Kinsey, Alfred C., Wardell Baxter Pomeroy, and Clyde E. Martin. 1948. *Sexual Behavior in the Human Male*. Philadelphia: Saunders.

Martin, Del. 1958. "Open Letter to Ann Aldrich." *The Ladder* (April): 4–6.

Martin, Del and Phyllis Lyon. 1972. *Lesbian/Woman*. San Francisco: Glide Publications.

Meaker, Marijane. 2003. *Highsmith: A Romance of the Fifties*. San Francisco: Cleis Press.

Meeker, Martin. 2005. "A Queer and Contested Medium: The Emergence of Representational Politics in the 'Golden Age' of Lesbian Paperbacks, 1955–1963." *Journal of Women's History* 17:1 (Spring):165–188.

Morgan, Claire. 1952. *The Price of Salt*. New York: W.W. Norton.

Nestle, Joan. 1992. *The Persistent Desire: A Femme-Butch Reader*. Boston: Alyson Books.

Packer, Vin. 2004. *Spring Fire*. [1952]. San Francisco: Cleis Press.

Stein, Gertrude. 1999. *Geography and Plays*. [1922]. Mineola, NY: Dover Books.

Stryker, Susan. 2001. *Queer Pulp: Perverted Passions from the Golden Age of the Paperback*. San Francisco: Chronicle Press.

Torres, Tereska. 2005. *Women's Barracks*. [1950]. New York: The Feminist Press at CUNY.

Villarejo, Amy. 1999. "Forbidden Love: Pulp as Lesbian History." In *Out Takes: Essays on Queer Theory and Film*, edited by Ellis Hanson. Durham, NC: Duke University Press.

Walters, Suzanna Danuta. 1989. "As Her Hand Crept Slowly Up Her Thigh: Ann Bannon and the Politics of Pulp." *Social Text* 23 (Fall-Winter):83–101.

Wilhelm, Gale. 1935. *We Too Are Drifting*. New York: Random House.

"The Wolfenden Report." 1957. Time Magazine Sept 16:39–40.

WSQ: Gender and Culture in the 1950s. 33: 3/4 (Fall/Winter 2005): entire issue.

Zimet, Jaye. 1999. *The Art of Lesbian Pulp Fiction, 1949–1969*. New York: Viking Studio Books.

The Feminist Press at the City University of New York is a nonprofit literary and educational institution dedicated to publishing work by and about women. Our existence is grounded in the knowledge that women's writing has often been absent or underrepresented on bookstore and library shelves and in educational curricula—and that such absences contribute, in turn, to the exclusion of women from the literary canon, from the historical record, and from the public discourse.

The Feminist Press was founded in 1970. In its early decades, the Feminist Press launched the contemporary rediscovery of "lost" American women writers, and went on to diversify its list by publishing significant works by American women writers of color. More recently, the Press's publishing program has focused on international women writers, who remain far less likely to be translated than male writers, and on nonfiction works that explore issues affecting the lives of women around the world.

Founded in an activist spirit, the Feminist Press is currently undertaking initiatives that will bring its books and educational resources to underserved populations, including community colleges, public high schools and middle schools, literacy and ESL programs, and prison education programs. As we move forward into the twenty-first century, we continue to expand our work to respond to women's silences wherever they are found.

For a complete catalog of the Press's 250 books, please refer to our website: www.feministpress.org.